HOW TO HANDLE
LONELINESS

You can stop searching, beause
this book is not only about
LONELINESS it is a revelation
of GOD's care for mankind and
how you can find help in every
way. It contains answers you have
been searching for all your life.

HOW TO HANDLE
LONELINESS

DR. SELVON SEEBRAN

ARPress
ILLUMINATING IDEAS
EMPOWERING VOICES

ARPress
45 Dan Road Suite 5
Canton, MA 02021
Hotline: 1(888) 821-0229
Fax: 1(508) 545-7580

Ordering Information:
Quantity sales. Special discounts are available on quantity purchases by corporations,associations, and others. For details, contact the publisher at the address above.

Printed in the United States of America.

ISBN-13:   Softcover   979-8-89330-966-9
              eBook   979-8-89330-967-6

Library of Congress Control Number: 2022902965

DEDICATION

THIS BOOK IS DEDICATED IN MEMORY OF MY LATE WIFE SHERRY SEEBRAN WHO DEPARTED THIS LIFE ON NOVEMBER 30TH, 2020. HER LOVE AND FAITHFULNESS TO GOD AND ME WILL NEVER BE FORGOTTEN. SHE IS NOW IN HEAVEN WITH JESUS REAPING HER REWARDS.

GOD'S BLESSINGS BE UPON YOU ALL

CONTENTS

INTRODUCTION

Spanning fifty years of ministry, and having preached and ministered, to hundreds of thousands of people in fifty countries of the world. The primary reason for writing this book resulted from years of observation and counseling with thousands of people who suffer from loneliness. I aim to present to you, the reader, the victims, causes, and most importantly, the solution concerning this nationwide as well as worldwide crisis.

This book was not written for literary style, but for the sole purpose of helping men and women, young people and children from all walks of life to overcome the problem and diabolical sickness of loneliness. Loneliness is a very big problem. It is a psychological, physiological, complicated problem, a real sickness that should not be treated lightly.

I would like the readers to understand that after months of research, I have discovered that there have been many attempts to deal with this sensitive issue. Statements of facts and figures were presented or written, nonetheless, no solutions were mentioned to solve the problem. I came to the conclusion that loneliness is not just a natural problem but also a spiritual problem and must be dealt with first spiritually and then socially. Because of this acute problem, millions of people are hurting. The facts and figures mentioned in this book are not meant to magnify the problem of loneliness, but instead, to enlighten your understanding as to the root cause of this problem.

I endeavor to reach people from all walks of life, including religious and non-religious people. Christians and non-Christians whom I know suffer from loneliness. Whether you agree with my strong Christian principles or not, please read this book with an open heart and mind and maintain this attitude: "The author wants to help you."

Loneliness does exist and if you are suffering from this complicated sickness, this book is designed to help you to face this problem head on, most of all to overcome the loneliness you are going through

All proceeds from sales go towards our
"Seven Point Outreach Program
Around The World"
See Website –
selvonseebranministries.org
Email
worldwidedeliverance@yahoo.com

LONELINESS DEFINED
CHAPTER ONE:
WHAT IS LONELINESS?

What is loneliness? Loneliness does not refer to being alone for a specific purpose but relating to loneliness itself.

After much research, it has been discovered that there are three major types of loneliness:

(1) *Transient Loneliness* – Very little attention has been given to this type of loneliness, which lasts for one to five hours.

(2) *Situational Loneliness* - This type of loneliness is the result of moving to another city, experiencing divorce, death of a loved one, separation from family and/or loved ones for a long period of time.

(3) *Persistent or Chronic Loneliness* - This is the worst type of loneliness, most referred to as the disease of loneliness.
This is a severe problem affecting millions of people.

Whatever type of loneliness you may be experiencing, the fact is, it is loneliness. One of America's greatest entertainers who passed away some years ago suffered from severe loneliness. I heard him make this statement: "I am one of the loneliest men in the world".

For most people suffering from this disease, just mention the mention of the word 'loneliness' contributes greatly to emotional distress.

What is this complicated, insidious, wonderland sickness call loneliness and what does it mean? A popular movie star and businessman said these words "I am healthy and possess millions of dollars, my name is on almost every billboard of the movies I made, I have a beautiful family, but what is this empty feeling that I have inside me night and day, is there an answer"? For most people suffering from this disease, just the mention of the word "loneliness" contributes greatly to emotional distress. What is this complicated, insidious wonderland sickness called loneliness and what does it mean?

First and foremost, loneliness is a feeling of emptiness, separation, isolation and a sense of being left out due to the above-mentioned reasons. A victim of loneliness feels destitute and deprived and craves compassionate attention from anyone. Loneliness constitutes a destructive form of self-pity, the feeling of being left out, forgotten, unattended, or ignored. It is akin to an empty space, a void within an individual that cannot be satisfied.

Loneliness is a feeling of unworthiness coupled with uselessness. to an certain extent, it is similar to feeling dead although alive; it is like the spirit of death within your being lowered within the depths of despair. Its helpless sufferer looks, seeks, and searches for fulfillment but to no avail. A certain man once said, "I am so lonely I could die."

Imagine if you would that you are in the center of the ocean, alone, in the middle of the night. You are trying, with every ounce of energy to swim ashore, but with each stroke you say to yourself I wonder if I am going to make it. I'm in the middle of the ocean! Then reality strikes you in the pit of your stomach and you convince yourself that there is no way you can make it; you will die out here in this ocean. To some extent this is how loneliness hits millions of people who experience loneliness night and day.

Loneliness is the most miserable feeling there is in life. It is a feeling of purposeless, useless, and aimless leaves one depressed and full of self-pity. Many lonely individuals take the "I do not care if no one cares" attitude. These individuals want to be loved but have no one to love and do not receive any love. Here's an illustration of loneliness: about twenty-five years ago, my wife and three children, and I were in Tennessee conducting Bible meetings. we were driving through the winding roads of the blue Tennessee Mountains one misty morning as the sun burst through the clouds, shining on the hills and valleys, and the smell of fresh country air filled our nostrils. We were on our way to visit the "Lost Sea" which is located above the town of Sweetwater, Tennessee.

When we arrived, to our surprise there were about 100 people who had the same idea we had. We parked our car and walked towards the gate of the "Wonder" as the natives call it. We purchased our tickets then a guide came and instructed us on certain safety rules. We then started our descent, hundreds of feet down into the depths of the earth. Down and down, we went and to our surprise, there was a lake hidden deep down in the depths of the mountain. This sight was both frightful and awesome at the same time.

Wonder and amazement saturated our being. The sight of seeing this lake of water in the depths of the earth beneath this mountain with all types of fish swimming was truly amazing. On our way up, (about 50 feet), the guide shouted out "Does anyone want to see and experience what real darkness is?" Everyone in the tour party shouted, "Yes!"

The guide told us to stand right where we were on the spiral steps wedged inside the mountain. He told us to hold on to one another and not to move an inch. He then pulled the switch that controlled the lighting within the cave of the mountain. This is the first time in my life that my family and I experienced real darkness. We could not even see anyone's teeth, or my own hand. In a way loneliness is extreme darkness all by itself.

Speak to anyone that is lonely and he or she will tell you in a heartbeat that it is the most indescribable feelings. Whenever I speak or minister to a lonely person, he or she concludes, "I am just downright lonely. Is there any help for a person like myself?" Upon embarking the task of writing this book time was taken to speak to dozens of people on the subject of their loneliness. As they spoke, they asked that their names be withheld, and rightfully, I do so with respect.

A certain young man experienced the divorce of his parents as a child. The kind of life that he had to live was completely unstable and his life was filled with uncertainties. He lived with one relative after another, then to an orphan home. "At this stage of my life" the twenty-one-year-old said, "I hate my parents, I am so lonely I wish I had never been born."

These are the words that came out of the mouth of a prostitute after turning her life over to God, with tears streaming down her heavily make-up face: "My parents turned their backs on me when I was fourteen years old. The loneliness and frustration inside of me drove me away from the confinements of relatives and friends into the streets at the age of twelve but thank God for his love to me regardless of what I have done in the past. I feel a hundred times better."

A certain thirty-year-old lady from Arkansas who lost her husband at the age of forty-two said "I have run through three divorces within a period of two years because I became so lonely and empty. How could these men have treated me like they did? I am so lonely and destitute. I am empty and do not know where to go, or who to turn to. I hate my life."

"I wondered if I made the right choice in life," cried a traveling salesman. "Every week I am away from home, leaving my wife and three children behind. Each week I become so lonely, I wish the airplane I am flying in would just drop or crash so this tormenting feeling of loneliness would end and my life could be over with. Perhaps then my wife and children could find someone else that could make them happy." Another man said, "I walk the parks and the streets, I sit in the restaurants. At times, I walk and hitchhike for miles upon miles. Even when people surround me, I cannot figure what this feeling is that haunts me day and night is. At night, I find a place where I have no choice but to be alone, I gaze and at the stars and repeatedly ask myself these questions: "Who am I, why do I have to live like this, and do I have to go through this wretched felling of loneliness the rest of my life?"

Loneliness makes people go where they do not want to go and do things they really do not want to do. Here are the words of an individual who was on the brink of emotional despair: "I was so lonely, I came out of my apartment and walked to one of the largest bridges in a popular city of America. During this walk, I saw people walking in the same direction with me, yet no one knew what I was going through. Hundreds of suggestions raced through my mind as to what I needed to do to alleviate this taunting, tormenting gut wrenching feeling that I was experiencing.

The last feat of despair took its toll within me, suggesting for me to do what so many others had done: jump off this bridge. I actually created the impression that I was just enjoying the view from the bridge, but when I saw the opportunity to be alone to jump over the bridge to finish my own life, an older man literally came out of nowhere and grabbed me. This saintly old gentleman said, "Son, please, you are too young to die." He took the time to speak words of wisdom into my life and those words changed the course of my life forever.

After what I call a divine appointment, I stopped a taxi and went back to my apartment, knelt down and prayed a prayer to God; He gave me the will to live.

People who are lonely describe their life as painful, depressed, hopelessness, despair, deep down sorrow, burdensome, hopelessness and suicidal. For them, it is a shadow that follows them all the time and rears its ugly head in so many ways. Loneliness can also be described as a deep down feeling of being lost. A person that is lonely can be in a state of mind that they want to be alone, but not really want to be alone, and I do not want to bother anyone else with the problems that I am carrying, but it would be certainly nice to have someone I can talk to.

Reminiscing certainly is a sign of loneliness. From the age of accountability which means children as far back they can remember, would be reminiscent about parent's problems, squabbles, fights, hurtful words and possibly separation and divorce. They carry these memories into adulthood which can initiate a life of loneliness if not helped. A sure sign of loneliness is worry, moping over past mistakes, failures. I am not accomplishing anything, and I am getting nowhere and do not know where I am heading.

Lonely people carry a guilt complex with a self-condemning self-inflicted attitude, at the same time sometimes blaming others for their mistakes. This of course goes with self condemnation, thus lonely people become withdrawn, difficult to understand most of the time, and at times hard to get along with. Here begins a journey into a life of loneliness. Even on sunny days and beautiful nights said an individual conversing with someone else "I am so down and sad, a doom and gloom feeling is always following me, I cannot seem to get rid of it,

CHAPTER TWO:
THE HIGHEST RATED EMOTIONAL SICKNESS

Loneliness is one of the most complicated, diabolical, and detrimental sicknesses, which has crept in unnoticed and undetected. Without a doubt, it is destroying millions of Americans and other people of the world. Aids, cancer, leukemia, muscular dystrophy, heart disease, and many other major sicknesses and diseases are being given first-hand attention by the United States government. Every health organization in America and Canada deals with every other kind of sicknesses and problems because it is seen; however, loneliness is hardly seen and dealt with because loneliness cannot be seen.

Believe it or not, based on a cross-country survey of a cross section of America, it is estimated that fifty to sixty million people—as much as a quarter of the population experience loneliness. This survey was conducted among all ages, in and among all classes and races of people. A leading newspaper reported that loneliness strikes as much as one in every three Americans. This figure might be applied to other countries such as Canada, Japan, China, India, Africa, South America, Middle East, Pakistan, Ethiopia and thousands of other countries of the world.

Loneliness affects families; this means husbands, wives, children living under one roof, friends, neighbors, business associates, office workers, neighbors, business associates, office workers, and others may surround people at home or in the workplace in an attempt to comfort the sufferers of loneliness. This can generally be applied to people in all positions and all other means of successful living.

The most populated cities of America and other parts of the world can never escape the miserable feeling of loneliness. Loneliness is inescapable, and has been expressed in music, literature, and art. Seventy percent of the songs that are aired on television, radio, or the Internet express loneliness. To feel lonely is to join the rest of humanity in acknowledging that we are separated from each other with a variety of different emotions pertaining to the problem.

One of the worst things that any human being could do is to entertain, accommodate and be insolvent about the problems he or she is experiencing. To choose to be lonely can spell disaster if there's no pursuit to resolve the problem of loneliness.

The loneliness syndrome is rapidly growing. The percentage of people who are suffering from loneliness can be clearly seen by the response to the amount of social activities and sporting events, including other social institutions that are mostly filled with people. People desperately try to help others alleviate theirs or someone else's loneliness. More than any other time in history, psychiatrists are doing a lucrative and brisk business. Seventy percent of their patients acknowledge loneliness as their chief complaint. Strange as it may seem, most patients in the hospitals and other medical institutions are not as sick as they claim to be rather, their main problem is loneliness even though they might not recognize it.

Loneliness is the highest rated emotional sickness of the century; feelings of loneliness affect thirty-six percent of Americans at the present time. One out of seven people say they frequently feel lonely. One out of four claim to be lonely. One out of two people whose life has been disrupted by separation, divorce, or death of a loved one, admitted to a dire and deep feeling of loneliness. Surprisingly, forty-five percent of married people confess to loneliness. An average of one out of four people have friends, but expressed they would like to have more friends. One out of ten or more people meet two or three times a week at discussion groups and the conversation is centered on their problems. Seventy percent of the discussion is focused on the loneliness they are experiencing. The most popular activity among friends today is giving mutual support. Most call on friends or visit one another's homes. Thirty percent perform favors, eat out regularly and rely on friends to fill their emotional needs, but even with all of this, some cannot understand why they are still lonely.

Approximately forty to forty-five percent of single adults who have never been married experience loneliness. These people openly admitted to experiencing extreme and severe loneliness. Then as the divorce rate rises each year, loneliness has become an accepted problem for an increasing number of men and women. This sickness obviously has a chain reaction of frustration and embarrassment. Most of all, if people are not helped, they are doomed to face a lifetime of loneliness.

Surprisingly, teenagers and children are rated as the highest percent of victims of loneliness. Overall, when divorce or some other problem occurs, senior citizens and older people rate the highest.

After much research, it was discovered that when this said group of people who, after giving their lives, time, money and energy to their children reached the age referred to as "elderly," they had to be sent to nursing homes or some other kind of institution. Many of these people die, going to their grave lonely. Words fail to express the respect and honor that I have for people of this age. "We have not seen our children in years" expressed an older couple and blurted out, "I guess we are not useful anymore." Aside from family and friends, there are a number of growing support groups to help cope with loneliness and its causes.

Self-help and support groups cater to thirty percent of singles, including that are divorced. According to a recent poll, people who suffer from loneliness are more likely to attend support groups. Nine percent said they are looking for more friends because they are lonely.

Loneliness is a problem it is a huge problem and growing daily. It is a disease that should not be treated lightly. Because of this acute problem, millions of people are hurting in America as well as in other countries of the world. However, divorcing and finding a new spouse or partner can never abate loneliness. The same is applied to people who are looking for pleasure, satisfaction, love and peace, some by traveling to the ends of the earth. People are trying everything under the sun to alleviate the pain but to their disappointment always go away empty.

Whether we would like to agree with this or not, loneliness is a universal problem. It visits every human soul (the reason is mentioned in Chapter Six) at some time in every culture, race, class, and age, and at all times in human history.

CHAPTER THREE:
THE ORIGIN OF LONELINESS

The author is definitely not trying to force his godly beliefs (note I did not say religious) on anyone. I wish I could, but in order for you to be helped, there are some godly facts you might have to face, so I ask kindly to read the following pages with an open heart and mind.

The attitude I would like you to maintain in reading the next few chapters can be explained in this manner: if you are eating fish and you bite into a bone, you will spit out the bone but continue eating the fish. The same principle applies here as you read, if there are some things the author wrote about that the reader might not understand, just keep on reading. What you will discover is amazing and beneficial to you in every way.

Whether you believe in the Bible or not, the author wants to encourage the reader to be open-minded. Personally speaking, the author has a strong faith in God, who is the Creator of all things, as you probably surmise by now. The Word of God—The Bible—backs up the author's belief and share a personal experience and relationship with God through His Son Jesus Christ.

The author has faith in God and bases his faith on the teachings of Jesus Christ recorded in *Matthew, Mark, Luke* and *John*. The author gains inspiration from reading the *Psalms*, *Proverbs* and of course the teachings and instructions of the Apostles recorded in the New Testament. The life, ministry, miracles, love and compassion of Jesus Christ Jesus Christ for humanity motivate the author to minister and help people in every way. The main purpose of this book is to help people who suffer from loneliness and other problems.

The first five books of Moses are awesome especially the book of *Genesis* from which I am now going quote from, to prepare the reader to deal with and handle loneliness. The Garden of Eden was home to our first parents, Adam and Eve who were created by God Himself. Eden was indeed every inch a real paradise. The sun shone with its multicolor rays shining through the beautiful trees, the gentle breeze blew as it carried the fresh scent of blossoming fruit trees and flowers throughout the atmosphere. Three winding rivers flowed graciously with clean, clear water, flowing graciously as the large green trees enhanced the river's banks.

In Eden the birds sang, each of them making a different sound in unison as they praised and worshipped God. Animals of every kind mingled and leisurely reclined under the shade of the widespread beautiful trees and nibbled from the grass and herbs. Beauty, grandeur, and pageantry filled the Garden of Eden. Most of all, everything was honored with the company of God's prized creation: Adam and Eve. They were granted power and dominion over everything from God. Adam tended the Garden and his wife; Eve was his helper. The magnificence and splendor within Eden were crowned with a mist that covered the entire garden. God gave Adam and Eve His best to enjoy and provided them with everything to satisfy their physical and spiritual needs.

As we zero into the cure for loneliness in the following chapters and paragraphs, you will realize that Adam and Eve had everything at their disposal to care for their physical needs, but what was it that comforted and completely satisfied their innermost being, their spirit?

"And they heard the voice of the LORD God walking
in the garden in the cool of the day: and Adam and his wife
hid themselves from the presence of the LORD God amongst
the trees of the garden." Genesis 3:8

From this Scripture, we understand that God came down in the cool of the day which was morning and evening and communed with Adam and Eve. God had very intimate fellowship with them; they were His most cherished creation. Adam and Eve had the privilege and opportunity of sharing their love, worship, praise, and adoration to God as they thanked Him for creating them.

They also expressed their appreciation for His abundant blessings. This was called "holy communion." Adam and Eve had a one-on-one, face-to-face, tangible, living relationship with God. In order for Adam and Eve to be satisfied, and their innermost yearning and inherent deep desire for God to be totally fulfilled, God Himself had to come down from heaven and spend time with them. They had to feel and see his immediate presence. Such holy communication alleviated the emptiness and loneliness within their spirit and imparted to them a sense of divine fatherly companionship. Simply stated, God's plan for Adam and Eve was to know Him and to have immediate access to Him, (God).

In order for Adam and Eve to be satisfied, and their innermost yearning to be complete, God visited them daily. Adam and Eve had a vibrant daily relationship with God. This was God's plan for mankind from the beginning.

Our first parents were also crowned with the Shekinah glory of God. The word "Shekinah" comes from the Hebrew word "*Kvod*" or "*Kabod*", Greek "*doxa*" means "to be covered with the light of the effulgence of God's presence", "to be covered with the fullness of the Presence of God" The prophet, Moses, experienced this when he came down from the mountain after being with God. The Shekinah glory shone so vibrantly on his face that he had to conceal his face from the people, it was too much for them to behold. When God created Adam and Eve, they were covered with the Shekinah glory of God from head to toe. You must understand that there was no sin, sickness, trouble, heartache, pressure, or loneliness and other problems. And a mist covered their nakedness.

Our first parents had longevity of earthly life; Adam and Eve were perfect in every way. Most of all, their inner being was totally satisfied. In order for you to alleviate or to be set from loneliness it must be realized that God's presence and power through the working of the Holy Spirit dwelling within your spirit gives total satisfaction. Procreation, this means God gave two human beings, (a man and a woman in marriage) the power of pro-creation; this is the miracle of bringing forth another human being into the world.

This means every human being should have a deep inherent desire and yearning for God. It can be safely said that God placed within every human being a spirit to desire and be satisfied with God.

When human beings replace God with everything else, this is where loneliness and other destructive forces invade the lives of human beings. When God is missing, "this is the origin of loneliness".

Adam and Eve relation communion and fellowship with God, well! You might think that something this wonderful and good would not last long? You are right: At this point, I am going to show you step by step how sin, sickness, evil, and loneliness originated. Before treating a patient, a true doctor must first deal with the root cause of a sickness, then proceed to obtain the cure. This is an allegory as to how I approach and deal with the problem of loneliness.

Before God made everything, Satan was already cast out from heaven. Prior to his eviction, like all other angels, Satan had the power of choice.

For those of you, who do not know of this dramatic event, allow me to take you to the Scripture, where   we find the record of Satan's rebellion against God?

Hell from beneath is moved for thee to meet thee at
thy coming: it stirred up the dead for thee, even all the chief
ones of the earth; it hath raised up from their thrones all the
kings of the nations.

All they shall speak and say unto thee,
Art thou also become weak as we? art thou become like unto us?

Thy pomp is brought down to the grave, and the noise of
thy viols: the worm is spread under thee, and the worms
cover thee.

How art thou fallen from heaven, O Lucifer, son
of the morning! how art thou cut down to the ground, which
didst weaken the nations!

For thou hast said in thine heart,
I will ascend into heaven, I will exalt my throne above the
stars of God:

I will sit also upon the mount of the congregation,
in the sides of the north: I will ascend above the heights
of the clouds; I will be like the most High. Yet thou shalt be
brought down to hell, to the sides of the pit.

They that see thee shall narrowly look upon thee, and consider
thee, saying, is this the man that made the earth to tremble, that did shake
kingdoms;

*That made the world as a wilderness, and
destroyed the cities thereof; that opened not the house of his
prisoners? KJV" Isaiah 14:9-17*

Satan was already on earth when God made Adam and Eve, and his sole purpose was to pervert and destroy God's creation. Because Adam and Eve were the only creatures created in the image of God, their spirit and soul were designed to last forever, and Satan was jealous of that. The same is applied to every human being that would be born of, and through Adam and Eve. Satan's purpose was to ruin and impregnate his evil nature in Adam and Eve, and the entire to be human race. The devil entered into the serpent, which walked on two legs. The serpent approached Eve and convinced her that God did not mean what He said about no one must touch or partake of the forbidden fruit in the midst of the Garden of Eden. The entire account of the fall of mankind is recorded in the Bible from the book of *Genesis 3:1-7*:

*"Now the serpent was more subtle than any beast of the field which the
LORD God had made. And he said unto the woman,*

*Yea, hath God said, Ye shall not eat of every tree of the garden? And the
woman said unto the serpent,*

*We may eat of the fruit of the trees of the garden: But of the fruit of
the tree, which is in the midst of the garden, God hath said,
Ye shall not eat of it, neither shall ye touch it, lest ye die.*

*For God doth know that in the day ye eat thereof, then
your eyes shall be opened, and ye shall be as gods, knowing
good and evil.*

*And when the woman saw that the tree was
good for food, and that it was pleasant to the eyes, and the tree
to be desired to make one wise, she took of the fruit thereof,*

16

*and did eat, and gave also unto her husband with her; and
he did eat.*

*And the eyes of them both were opened, and they
knew that they were naked; and they sewed fig leaves together,
and made themselves aprons.*

*Eve listened to the devil; she looked and saw that the fruit in the midst of
the Garden was good. Then the devil seduced Eve into disbelieving God's
Word. She partook and ate the fruit and Adam did the same. From that
point on mankind had to deal with the problem of sin and its results.*

*"And they heard the voice of the LORD God walking
in the garden in the cool of the day: and Adam and his wife
hid themselves from the presence of the LORD God amongst
the trees of the garden.*

*And the LORD God called unto Adam, and said unto him, Where art
thou? And he said, I heard thy voice in the garden, and I was
afraid, because I was naked; and I hid myself. And he said, who told thee
that thou wast naked?*

*Hast, thou eaten of the tree, whereof I commanded
thee that thou shouldest not eat?*

And the serpent said unto the woman, Ye shall not surely die:

*For God doth know that in the day ye eat thereof, then
your eyes shall be opened, and ye shall be as gods, knowing*

*And when the woman saw that the tree was good for food, and that it was
pleasant to the eyes, and a tree to be desired to make one wise, she took of
the fruit thereof, and did eat, and gave also unto her husband with her;
and he did eat.*

And the eyes of them both were opened, and they knew that they were naked; and they sewed fig leaves together and made themselves aprons."
Genesis 3:1-7

Eve listened to the devil; she looked and saw that the fruit in the midst of the Garden was good. Then the devil seduced Eve into disbelieving God's Word. She partook and ate the fruit and Adam did the same. From that point on, mankind has to deal with the problem of sin and its results.

And they heard the voice of the LORD God walking
in the garden in the cool of the day: and Adam and his wife
hid themselves from the presence of the LORD God amongst
the trees of the garden.

And the LORD God called unto Adam,
and said unto him, Where art thou? And he said, I heard thy
voice in the garden, and I was afraid, because I was naked;
and I hid myself.

And he said, Who told thee that thou wast naked? Hast thou
eaten of the tree, whereof I commanded thee that thou shouldest not eat?

And the man said, The woman whom thou gavest to
be with me, she gave me of the tree, and I did eat. And the
LORD God said unto the woman,

What is this that thou hast done? And the woman said,
The serpent beguiled me, and I did eat. And the LORD God said unto the
serpent, because thou hast done this, thou art cursed above all cattle, and
above every beast of the field; upon thy belly shalt thou go, and dust shalt
thou eat all the days of thy life:

And I will put enmity between thee and the woman, and between thy seed and her seed; it shall bruise thy head, and thou shalt bruise his heel.

Unto the woman he said, I will greatly multiply thy sorrow and thy conception; in sorrow thou shalt bring forth children; and thy desire shall be to thy husband, and he shall rule over thee.

And unto Adam he said, because thou hast hearkened unto the voice of thy wife, and hast eaten of the tree, of which I commanded thee, saying,

Thou shalt not eat of it: cursed is the ground for thy sake; in sorrow shalt thou eat of it all the days of thy life; Thorns also and thistles shall it bring forth to thee; and thou shalt eat the herb of the field.

In the sweat of thy face shalt thou eat bread, till thou return unto the ground; for out of it wast thou taken for dust thou art, and unto dust shalt thou return. And Adam called his wife's name Eve.

After Adam and Eve sinned against God, God cursed the serpent, which affected its original creation or form. Instead of walking like a human being, it was reduced to crawling on its belly and eating dirt the rest of its life. The curse of sin also affected the animal kingdom. They became ferocious and began to eat one another. As for the earth, it began to grow thorns and thistles.

The entire earth was cursed and sometime later, caused a cataclysmic earthquake, which split the earth and caused the land to separate, forming different continents, countries, and islands. Viewing the earth from thousands of feet from an airplane, one must realize that something unusual had to happen in order for the earth to be like it is. The curse of sin adversely affected every living thing God created including the earth, forestry, trees, flowers, and vegetation. Life and land were not the same way as in the beginning when God first made everything.

Adam and Eve felt the effects of the curse of sin more than all of God's creation. God's original plan for the woman bringing forth children (without pain) but after Eve disobeyed God, childbirth would be with pain. Man's original life of relaxation, joy, peace, contentment and happiness was interrupted because of the decision to disobey God.

From where did loneliness originate? After Adam and Eve sinned and death entered into the world, the human race was plunged into total disarray and confusion. Mankind became so wicked that they began to intermingle with demons and beasts, birthing a type of unnatural beings resembling demons and beasts.

> *"So He (God) drove them out from the Garden of Eden."*
> *Genesis 3:23.*

Loneliness is primarily caused by a life without God. All types of loneliness, including chronic loneliness, originated when mankind forfeited the presence of God in Eden.

CHAPTER FOUR:
CAUSES OF LONELINESS

Is it possible to be lonely in a crowd of thousands of people? Yes, it is! Loneliness is an introverted, individual problem that millions face and fight each day.

Each day people hustle, bustle, and drive bumper to bumper in traffic going to his or her workplace in cities across America. These very same people who look forward going to work in the morning, staying at the workplace or office all day, some of them dread going back home in the evening to face their loneliness for another night. In the minds of some individuals, going to work is the best thing that can happen to some of them, because it seemingly relieves their feelings of loneliness and distracts them from their problems.

"I dread going home in the evening," said one man. "As soon as I get home, I flip the television on and try to fix some dinner. Then I sit down to eat while flipping through 100 channels but none of them can remove the tormenting feelings that I face night after night."

Certain symptoms precede every type of sickness and problem that exist in the world today. The root cause must be found before there can be a cure. Think of it in these terms: in order for electricity to get to your house, it must first be harnessed then directed through power units, generators, and poles. Finally, it is hooked up to the wires, light fittings and bulbs. Only then will it supply light to your homes, offices, and places of business. Here's another scenario: an Airplane cannot fly without power. The dynamics of that entire airplane is caused by a small computer chip within the center of the Plane's mechanism which triggers the jets that **causes** it to operate and fly.

Loneliness is caused by a majority of major problems; the source of loneliness starts because of certain problem or problems and escalates into larger issues. The main cause of loneliness will be explained in depth in the next few chapters, nonetheless, there are other insurmountable problems existing within the lives of millions of people which causes and lead to loneliness.

It's important to understand that a person can choose to be alone for some specific purpose; for instance, to concentrate on a project or an invention, to rest, recuperate, study, or pray. This is just the opposite of what this book is referring to. It is dealing with people who suffer from the complicated sickness called loneliness, not people who desire to be alone for healthy reasons.

Freddy and Mary were a couple respected by everyone in the community where they lived. They had three children and several grandchildren; they were successful in life and had a happy home and family. But Freddy, who looked healthy for his age, had a massive heart attack and died. This was a great shock to his wife. After the funeral their children family and friends left for their respective homes. It was then that the shock of her husband dying settled in, from this point onward Mae said "the thought of her husband being dead and gone for good, she could not become adjusted of her husband death for years. Each night hundreds of thoughts would race through her head, was I guilty in anyway causing his sudden death? Did I do my best for him while he was alive? Was I ugly or nice to him? Maybe I should have done better or did I fail to do my best.

She repeatedly refused any kind of professional counsel and as a result, suffered from a severe case of depression and chronic loneliness. Six months after her husband's death, Mary died of grief and most of all, loneliness.

These true stories can be an incentive to encourage people in simi lar situations to seek professional and spiritual help which means a better life and longevity.

Death of a loved one can cause loneliness in its worst stage.

Many widowed men and women of whom you see every day suffer from loneliness above all else. Losing a loved one can be very devastating especially if a couple was married for many years. The Bible specifically states that much attention should be given to widows. Most of these people have forgotten how to smile. Studies indicate that loneliness victims suffer so much more where the climate is colder because they are not out and about as much enjoying pleasant weather.

Divorce of a loved one is a major cause of loneliness.

Every one out of five marriages end in divorce. Personally speaking, from the author's point of view divorce should not be the object or motive when problems arise in marriage, especially where children are involved. Whenever problems arise the word divorce should never be uttered from any of the spouse's mouth, please take each other's hands and pray over marital problems, and stay married. Where children are involved, more thought should be given and please consider your children because children suffer most with immense long-lasting depression and loneliness through out their lives, when their parents are divorced. Children have long lasting scars from their parent's divorces.

Divorce no matter what or how, none of the spouses are the same after divorce.

By the way what is it that the other man or woman has that you are thinking of remarrying, that your present wife or husband does not have. By God's help there is room to help each other, why divorce when you might be faced with same problem with the new wife or husband you are thinking about, by God's help make the marriage work.

Thousands of young people leave their parents' home each year in search of opportunities which they believe will bring them fame and fortune. Some of them are fortunate to have their dreams come true. But forty seven percent of these young people are disappointed in their quest for the bright lights. What some of them thought would bring them fame and fortune in most instances brought them shame and disappointments. Most young people who leave home end up in the hands of the wrong people; broke, busted, and beaten. Then they are forced to do things they do not want to do, such as pimping, prostituting, and or selling drugs. Most of all, they end up as lonely individuals. Some of them are too embarrassed to even go back home.

The author would take the opportunity right at this juncture to interject some Godly wisdom for parents. Almost each month more or less some adults, especially teenagers and children are being reported being missing from homes, schools and other places. There are some mentally deranged who are always on the lookout for young women, teenagers and children. Never provoke your loved one's teenagers and children. This of course means do not abuse them physically and verbally, this could drive them to run away from home and possibly into the hands of the wrong people and this possibly could be detrimental. Never give an opportunity for your children to be lonely children do not know how to cope in loneliness.

If in case a teenager or child runs away from home, or encounters problems in school, college or being away from home, some of them might make severe mistakes or your daughter becomes pregnant or your son gets busted do not threaten them, at the same time if they are runaways always keep the doors open, the lights on and open hearts for your children or loved ones. There are times that most parents are so taken up with everything else except the things that matter: Love, togetherness, showing you care combine with Bible reading, prayer, going to church, enjoying life in a pure clean manner would save a lifetime of loneliness and regrets.

Honor your father and mother which is the first commandment with promise, that you may live long on the earth, Fathers provoke not your children to wrath but bring them up the in nature and admonition of the Lord, Ephesians 6: 3-4.

While conducting revival meetings in Ft. Lauderdale, Florida, one of the tires on my car went flat. I pulled into a tire shop and the owner of the tire shop told me to have a seat while he fixes the tire. While waiting, I saw two school children came by the tire shop their ages were about eight and nine years old. They asked me if I would allow them to start breaking the nuts of the wheel. I was kind of surprised that these boys were not in school. Having a heart for children, I asked the owner of the tire shop if it was all right for them to help; he said it was. Those boys broke the nuts and pulled the tire off.

The attendant fixed the tire, and then the boys replaced the tire, tightening the bolts and everything else. I paid for the repair, but before I left, I had a good friendly conversation with those two boys. I asked them where their parents were and why they were not in school. They explained that they did not know where their parents were, and they had to fend for themselves.

The proprietor of the tire shop confirmed this to be true. I paid for the repair but before I left, I continued my conversation with the two boys; I told them that I was a minister or pastor as I spoke to them about God, how Jesus died on the cross for them, and instructed them to attend Sunday school. I reinforced my conversation with them and emphasized that they must attend school in order to better themselves, they listened intently. That morning in particular, it was kind of cold in Ft. Lauderdale. I noticed that one of the boys began leaning on my right side, edging closer and closer to me. I prayed with both of them, as I prayed this nine-year-old who was leaning on me got closer and closer, after I prayed with them, I gave them some money, they were astonished!

They couldn't believe that I did that. Then I heard the kid that was leaning on me said some words which brought tears to my eyes, and these were his words, "Mister, it was cold before you got here but while you were here it became so warm. I wish you were here with us with us all the time". After this experience even though the farther North I drove it became colder and colder, but the words of that little boy made my drive to Georgia warmer.

Millions of people are cold and lonely. The loneliness that people are going through is nothing compared to cold days and nights. But as Adam Eve found comfort, peace and solace when God came down in the garden of Eden and kept them company, talked and fellowship with them, in the same way you can experience God's warmth in your life. Always remember with God and with you HE CAN KEEP YOU WARM.

Life goes on as the young man or young lady goes off to college. Eventually, he or she meets someone, falls in love, gets married, then a family of their own. The parents miss their sons or daughters then, situational loneliness sets in. This type of loneliness harbors itself deep within the parents' hearts and they carry this burden all their lives. Some of course can become adjusted but in some way suffer from a mild form of loneliness. Although most parents who miss their children accept their absence as a way of life, others fall into deep despair and loneliness.

Being away from people you have become attached to.

The absence of family, loved ones, immediate friends, and relocating from one city to another is a primary cause of loneliness. "I can hardly handle this," exclaimed one man. "Why does it have to be this way?" Generally speaking, there are droves of men and women who travel thousands of miles each week just to fulfill their calling and make a living. Pilots, flight attendants, soldier's army personnel, ministers, and missionaries who must be away from home and their country for months or years suffer serious bouts of loneliness.

Sometimes I cannot help but notice the insensitivity of so many people in relation to foreigners coming to America from other countries. Except for the American Indians, everyone else came from somewhere. The freedom to come to this country is one attribute that makes America beautiful.

Americans travel to other countries of the world; most of the time when we travel overseas, the people in the host countries do everything possible to make us happy. On the other hand, when these same people arrive in the United States to work or make a living to better themselves, their family, Americans seldom return the favor of hospitality. Some foreigners are met with remorse, resentment and in turn loneliness sets in.

Once, after I concluded one of my revival meetings, I went into a restaurant to eat I noticed a man sitting by himself eating I could tell that he was from another country. As I looked at him, I couldn't help but notice the sad far away look in his eyes. Sensing his loneliness and discerning his need to talk to someone, I walked over his to his table and introduced myself to him. In turn, he requested that I sit and eat with him. After talking to him for a while he told me what country he was from, how long he had been in America, and then started to pour his heart out to me.

With tears in his eyes, he told me that he did not want to remain in America anymore. He said, "I had such high hopes coming to America. I thought everybody here was nice and friendly. I am so kind and helpful to people from America when they are in my country. I mistakenly thought everyone was a Christian. Even some of the ministers I met and entertained when they visited my country and home let me down and disappointed me. I just want to go back home." I spoke to him for a while and even invited him to my home. I had prayer with him after which he was so relieved that someone actually took the time just to speak to him.

With this book in mind, I spoke to about a dozen college and university students; every one of them confessed to experiencing a serious stretch of loneliness to the point of being depressed. One student confessed, "I am so lonely even though there are other students in this university; loneliness looms and haunts me night and day. I cannot understand what's wrong with me. "If I did not want to complete my studies and get somewhere in life, I would have already headed back home."

The men and women in the U.S. Army and all other military services who are stationed thousands of miles away from home suffer severe loneliness.

A certain salesman mentioned that due to the type work he does and travel thousands of miles each week, stays in some of the best hotels and motels he said, "From the time I check into the hotel, get the key and open the door, I get so lonely and frustrated I feel like kicking and breaking the windows wide open."

To Some Success can mean disaster at times.

America, unlike some countries is a great country to live in, however, the spirit to compete is so demanding, the obsession to get ahead and make ends meet is so pressuring, and that to fail in this country is a curse. Why? Because successful people especially celebrities, sports personalities and entertainers are placed on such high pedestals.

The result is that many people compare themselves to the media driven definition of success and become intimidated and carry an inferiority complex, because they are not as successful as those people who are placed on such a high pedestal. Such thinking has infected and affected millions. But a person who has knowledge and knows God and have faith in God does not allow this kind of thinking to rattle their minds.

Poverty and loneliness go hand in hand.

I have witnessed with my own eyes some of the poorest countries of the world and poverty is a curse. I had an experience that has left an indelible impression on me for many years. While overseas we conducted a revival meeting in a large soccer field. The following day we decided to take a drive in one of the poorest areas of that country. Words can hardly describe what I saw. After leaving the city my wife and I drove for about twenty-five miles, and then turned off the main highway we witness poverty to extreme level; most of the people had rags for clothing while others had no clothes on at all. One thing in particular that caught my attention was a mother who looked like skin and bones trying to nurse a baby who looked like skin and bones. Her mother's instinct was intact; she did not want her baby to die and was desperately trying to breastfeed the baby. My wife spoke to me and said with tears in her eyes, "This woman has nothing in her to feed the baby." My wife Sherry and I went to her and spoke to her about Jesus and explained the message of salvation through Jesus Christ. We prayed with her; only then we saw the far away look of loneliness in her eyes disappeared. Her face lit up and then she smiled.

After we ministered to her, I took out some money from my pocket and gave it to her. I instructed her to get a reliable person to go to the closest store (or shop as they call it) and buy some food for her and milk for the baby. She thanked me over and over because she knew somebody CARED.

You have heard the saying, "Sometimes it's lonely at the top" and to add to that! depressingly so. This might not surprise you but being a leader of a country is not an easy responsibility. I am referring to kings, queens, prime ministers, and leaders of different countries. Some of them are forced to smile for the news media and television cameras, but cameras can never reveal the turmoil that occurs on the inside of these public personalities. They have the unfortunate pressure of trying to please everyone knowing that they cannot, especially in America

When President Ronald Reagan was in office I saw a picture of him, he was standing and looking out from one of the White House windows. He was looking at the snow-covered grounds, the ice draped trees, the dark gray skies, and the still atmosphere. No other person was included in the picture. Underneath the photograph were these words: "A President's Job is a Lonely Job. Yes, it's Lonely at the Top."

The U.S. Virgin Islands is a tourist's paradise. I visited there and conducted some meetings. During these meetings, I liked to go out in the morning hours and meet people, check out their lifestyle, enjoy the beautiful scenery, look at the sunlight and the multicolor clear blue water, and even fish once in a while.

My evening hours were reserved for prayer, study, and ministry, and to meet the needs of the people. I remember one morning I decided to fish. I drove for about twenty miles and came to one of the most beautiful areas. I settled down to enjoy the beautiful scenery, and to fish. While fishing, about two hundred yards in front of me I noticed that the ocean became very boisterous and unusually bubbly. Believe me when I say that a bit of fear came over me as I was wondering what this was all about. Suddenly, I noticed a large U.S. submarine emerge out of the water. The hatch opened and officers came out of the submarine one by one. They got into a little boat and came towards the shore. After they all landed, I saw a very stately looking gentleman approaching me, to my surprise he had fishing gear in his hands as he introduced to me and began talking about being in a submarine month after month. To my delight, I found out that I was speaking to the captain of the submarine he was very simple.

I introduced myself told him that I was a minister. We spoke as we fished, and I was very curious and asked him during our conversation, "How does it feel to be hundreds of feet beneath the ocean, months at a time?" He replied, "It's no picnic being down there even though I am in the presence of other officers and men. It's one the eeriest, loneliest feelings in the world." We continued to dialog, and I discovered that he was from the state I live; Georgia. This made me feel right at home. While we fished, he said, "One of the greatest feelings being down there months at a time is to know God through Jesus Christ as Lord and Savior. It's the only way that I overcome loneliness."

Being rejected by others.

This is often a major cause of loneliness. The rejected group includes people who are ridiculed and/or abandoned by family, friends, fellow employees, or schoolmates. In some cases, rejection is instilled by verbal and psychological assaults. Individuals develop defensive walls in order to protect themselves from negative environments but in an attempt to shut out those who harm them, often close the door on people that can help them.

<u>Being hailed a misfit or a loser.</u>

We live in a society of the "greatness" mentality denoting that everyone must be great and wonderful in order to be seen as successful. This attitude is generated primarily from the media, universities, schools, and the sports world. Our society raves about the winners of sporting events over and over again, however, nothing is said about the other person or people who lost and were willing to compete and try their best. Looking at our society, an individual cannot but help think or feel that they must be perfect, be a winner, or be recognized. Sad to say, this kind of spirit has been perpetuated even in the church world. We view people on television or the big screen, and think, "Yes, he is really great, and man, he is really something."

Often, people are lonely and shut out, even of their own choosing, because of this philosophy. Believe me there are times in your life it is not that important what people thinks of you as an individual, but it is only that what God thinks of a person is important.

CHAPTER FIVE:
THE ROOT CAUSE OF LONELINESS

Before going any further, it must be realized that loneliness is not just a natural problem; it is a spiritual problem. In order for you to understand the root cause of loneliness, you must understand the total make up of human beings. I realize that this book will be read by people who are not Christians and do not believe in the Bible, however, if that's you, I ask you to please continue reading with an open heart and mind. Without a doubt, you have more to gain than lose.

My intent is to help people from every race, religion, and culture to understand the truth of God's word and the love that He has for each individual soul. In the book of *Genesis*, we find that mankind (mankind means men and women), was created in God's image and His likeness. Read what the Bible says:

> *"And God said, Let us make man in our image, after our likeness." Genesis 1:26*

> *"And the LORD God formed man of the dust of the ground, and breathed into his nostrils the breath of life; and man became a living soul." Genesis 2:7*

Mankind is a threefold being comprised of body, soul and spirit. A human being is a threefold being, and the most obvious of a human being is the body. The body is the part that you see first on a daily basis. Usually, when you look at a person, the first thing that catches your attention is their body, how they are dressed, the type of shoes on their feet, how they smell, whether they are tall, short, fat, skinny, and the color of his or her skin. All of which I might add does not make any difference in the sight of God.

In this day and time in which we live, so much attention is given to the body. Turn on the television and you will notice practically every channel has some kind of exercise or workout program being promoted, suggesting and encouraging good health.

Even on some commercials and other billboard advertisements, you notice how they use pictures of the human body, some happy, some suggestive, some professional, etc. The point that I am trying to make is that the emphasis constantly revolves around the body, the "outer shell", which is important. I am not insinuating that an individual be physically out of shape, but we have a generation of people who think that the body is the most important thing and spend thousands of dollars trying to keep in sync with what society dictates.

The author does not want to give the idea of writing a book for writing book's sake. But the fact of writing this book is obviously to communicate to the reader, especially those who suffer from loneliness and the other symptoms that follow this sickness. If the reader or anyone else will be helped, there must be clear understanding and wisdom to get help. If you do not mind, we are certainly going to do a bit of "Bible Study" right here! Again, this is with the intention to overcome loneliness and other related symptoms that follows the diabolical sickness of loneliness.

A human being is made of three parts, THE BODY, THE SPIRIT AND THE SOUL. The BODY is the "outer shell" (excuse me for putting it this way) but is the body the important thing? Yes, it is! The body is a house (in Christian terms the body is referred to as a Temple) the human body houses and accommodates the two most important parts of a human being. That is the SPIRIT AND THE SOUL.

Theologians' places the body first because the body is the first part of men and women that comes into view foremost. But there are two important parts of the body that the human eye does not see which is of utmost importance; this is THE SOUL AND THE SPIRIT.

Some theologians say the body, the spirit and the soul, this is also correct, but the author wants to interject the Bible's teaching of the body, soul and spirit just to bring you to point of dealing with loneliness. Here is the reason for stating THE BODY, THE SOUL AND THE SPIRIT, mentioning the SPIRIT LAST.

There are many words from the Hebrew language referring to the word BODY, but the Hebrew word that stands out for body is the word "*BASAR*". This Hebrew word refers to the entire human body and its functional capabilities. But this word also means flesh which is temporary and does not last forever. The Greek word for BODY is "*SOMA*", which means a transitory or temporary thing. Of course, the human body compositions are higher than the flesh of animals etc, but this Greek "*Soma*" word brings out the meaning that the body or flesh of a human. Which is obviously temporary?

The word SOUL derives from the Hebrew word "*NEPHESH*", or "*CHAYAH*", meaning whole person, the real you. It is distinct from the body, closely related to the spirit, (sometimes writers associate the soul and the spirit to be the same but according to research, this is not so.) The soul of every human being is the life itself, propagating the body and the spirit; in this modern day and time certain music derives a sort of music as "soul" from the word "soul", "you got soul" is this case what this word soul referring to "you got the real thing". The soul or souls are the real part of you. At death the soul departs from the body and enters into eternity with or without God, Heaven or Hell. *Hebrews 9:27.*

35

The word SPIRIT, theologians associate the soul and the spirit to be the same. But from research the spirit is slightly higher than the soul. The word "spirit" which comes from the Hebrew word "*RUACH*", which means breath of life or God's life, this also means life dependant upon another or where God dwells. The Greek word for SPIRIT is "*PUEMA*", which means breathe into.

In ancient Greek medicine "*puema*" is the form of circulating air necessary for the systematic functioning of the vital organs in the human body. This word '*PUEMA*' also means to breathe upon to survive. It must be understood that this paragraph is not with intent to down, condemn or be judgmental of an individual lifestyle, but this is with intent to help. Loneliness is the core reason why people try drugs, such as crack, cocaine, alcohol, and illicit pleasures and sex, party all night and craves the spotlight and power, it's because they are looking for something to replace the vacuum or empty space inside of them, and this is because the Spirit of God is missing within their being.

Originally an individual was made by God so God Spirit can dwell or live in the human spirit. God placed a Spirit within every human being that He created in order to connect mankind to Him and to satisfy mankind. This is how God created you and every other human being.

The Spirit is the immaterial part of you, which is slightly higher than the soul; this must be reiterated: it is the element in man placed there by God to desire, yearn, hunger (spiritually). And when God is not in the spirit of human beings, nothing or no other satisfies. The root cause of loneliness, in plain everyday simple language, is due to the absence of God from the spirit of man. That empty space or vacuum on the inside of you is there because God's Spirit is not dwelling in your spirit. We'll explore this truth in the next chapter.

Religion is the most important aspect in the lives of millions of people, religion is mankind's search for God, but it is not God's provision for mankind, especially in the search for peace, joy, satisfaction, and happiness. Why do you think so many people travel thousands of miles to shrines, sunrises, and so-called holy places, wash themselves in certain rivers, do good works, go through certain rituals, burn candles, keep holy days, observe moons and Sabbaths, and spend thousands of dollars to meet or shake hands with the head of certain religious organization? Why would people do that? Obviously, mankind is desperately searching and trying everything to satisfy them. But alas, there is a cry in human beings: they are searching for God.

Such quests and pursuits will not alleviate the loneliness or any other problems that we encounter because only God satisfies. Billionaires, millionaires, and other wealthy people, they would give any amount of money to get rid of their loneliness. They possess great sums of money and yet will do anything to satisfy their inner emptiness. They believe that their riches will satisfy their soul's deepest need. How deceptive riches are! But individuals who are rich can find peace, joy, real satisfaction in Jesus Christ, because of what He did on Calvary's Cross for us. And of course, riches and money can be used for the propagation of the Gospel of Jesus Christ which brings real peace, joy, real happiness and contentment. Combined with a program like ours to shelter the homeless, feed the hungry, clothe the naked help the poor and needy, love the loveless and of course reach millions of lonely people. *Matthew 25:31-46*

Most Americans are caught up in every type of entertainment, pleasure, and sporting event. Once the entertainment party's over, they are simply lonely. Again, I reiterate, the problem is: "God's Spirit is missing from many of His created children". Choice is powerful, choosing the wrong thing specifically and routinely causes many complex problems, situations and sicknesses that have plagued the human race. In the Bible, the book of Deuteronomy, we find these words:

"I call heaven and earth to record this day against you,
that I have set before you life and death, blessing and cursing:
therefore, choose life, that both thou and thy seed may live:" Deuteronomy
30:19

The United States government spends millions of dollars to stop the flow of drugs into this country, but this won't stop the lonely, empty feeling people have inside of them. Even people involved with different religions and or cultic movements are not at peace with themselves. People are just miserable, restless, tossed, and driven

By choosing God you will choose life, which is supernatural strength to live, for both you and your children. As I am writing, the news media is covering one of the most bizarre, and ill-fated cases of the death of one of America's celebrities: She was esteemed by many to be a beautiful woman and had recently given birth to a baby girl. Tragically, her death was preceded by the untimely death of her son who, before his demise, told his mother how lonely he was. This celebrity said "she even had dreams of her dead son who was quite unhappy and restless in the afterlife, (some truth) but oh! How the devil deceives the hearts and minds of those who do not believe in the true and Living God!

"In whom the god of this world hath blinded the minds
of them which believe not, lest the light of the glorious gospel
of Christ, who is the image of God, should shine unto them."
2 Corinthians 4:4

Certainly, I feel compassion for her (and her son), but with all her fame, money, and beauty, she wasn't satisfied or fulfilled. The news media reported that her death was caused by an accidental drug overdose but throughout her life, this celebrity made the ultimate wrong choice. She chose to live apart from God and therefore, God's Spirit was absent from her spirit. Speaking about choice or choices, this statement would surprise you, God Himself cannot choose for you? Yes, I know that some people will be amazed at this statement. When God created Lucifer, he was the head of the music ministry in Heaven. God also created the Angels; God gave them the power of choice. But Lucifer who is Satan exalted and rebelled against God, he was cast out of Heaven to the then known Earth. From that time to now the devil hates anything that is in the image of God or has God's name.

The same with Adam and Eve, when He created them in the Garden of Eden, He did give them the power of choice. But guess who was already on Earth? The devil, Eve made the wrong choice took the bait of what the devil suggested, so did Adam and both of them fell into the sin. By the choosing to disobey God they plunged the entire human race into sin, while the blame game goes on from that time to now. This is what is left, the empty space or vacuum on the inside of every human. But God already provided way for the space or emptiness on the inside of men and women to be filled and satisfied. But humans have the power of choice, please choose right and choose God and He will fill the emptiness on the inside of you. This of course can help solve the loneliness problem and a host of other problems.

CHAPTER SIX:
RESULTS OF LONELINESS

America has become a Mecca for every kind of religion, cult, and belief including voodoo, witchcraft, satanic worship, psychic readings and sorcerers. Illegal drugs have suddenly become a multibillion-dollar industry because people with other problems and those who suffer from loneliness are hooked and looking for more drugs to get a temporary high in an attempt to dispel the darkness of their soul.

Pleasure seekers invent and organize every new type of sporting event upon what we already have. But even with all of this new fanfare they are not satisfied. Never before in the history of this country have, we seen so many "lonely hearts" clubs. Recently, thousands have opened in an attempt to address the needs of lonely individuals. Single bars are in popular demand. Ever overcrowded, they attract thousands and thousands of people each day and night, and most of all the owners of these clubs are cashing in millions of dollars on people's loneliness. Soothsayers and psychics earn millions by luring people to believe that they have the answer to their problems when in fact they are taking advantage of people's loneliness.

Certain telephone companies are also cashing in millions of dollars. Because of the millions of people that are suffering from loneliness, special 800, 888, and 900 numbers are available for lonely people to call and talk to someone about their lives. In addition, these companies have people or recordings that are working around the clock, specializing in topics ranging from sex, drugs, and companionship that they offer for a certain price.

A certain tabloid newspaper advertised nine printed ads with names and numbers of psychic mediums, soliciting business from lonely people. This is not a secret business anymore. These operations are now on daily television programs. Psychiatrists, doctors, hospitals and other private institutions are conducting more business than at any other time in history. Psychiatrists report that fifty percent of their patients are lonely. Their clientele consists mostly of millionaires, movie stars, celebrities, middle class and a few poor people.

Loneliness affects a person physically, mentally, socially and of course, spiritually. People who suffer from loneliness can easily be lured into every type of vice, habit, illicit sex and ungodly pleasure, which can be very devastating. This disease of loneliness often results in many adverse conditions in an individual's life such as depression. Because of loneliness, multitudes of people go into months and months of depression.

Several years ago, I heard one of the most heart-rending stories I ever heard. I was scheduled to minister in a certain church in Memphis, Tennessee. The starting night for the meeting was on a Monday night. From Georgia I drove to Memphis and made it in good time. I settled in a hotel room then called the pastor to let him know that I was in town.

During our conversation, the pastor informed me that we could not start the meetings Monday night as planned. He explained that one of the ladies in the church had died. The pastor explained that the woman who died used to sit in the front pew. She was one of the happiest and most reliable members in the congregation. Then he proceeded to tell me how that after a few months, the very same woman who used to sit in the front pew started sitting on the back pew with a far away left out look in her eyes. He explained that during Sunday's meeting he made an effort to minister to this particular member of his congregation, but while en route to her he stopped to pray for someone else. By the time he finished praying, he looked for the lady to go and minister to her, but she had already left the service.

The very night that we were supposed to start the revival meeting, the pastor received a telephone call and was shocked to learn that very evening that same woman had committed suicide. Upon investigating why, she killed herself, he found out that her husband was unfaithful to her. Prior to finding out about her husband's unfaithfulness she felt forsaken and neglected. She then became very lonely and depressed and finally decided to end it all by taking her own life. With choked up emotion in his voice the pastor said he would never again take people for granted, that he would do everything possible to help a person when that person is in need.

Lonely people develop harmful habits that will destroy them in every way: physically, socially, spiritually and financially. According to a reliable source, an annual average of fifteen persons per every 100,000 commits suicide; Los Angeles ranks in the middle, about twenty-one percent per 100,000. In San Francisco, the average is even higher with a figure of forty percent of 100,000 people commit suicide. The report went on to state that young people seem to think that there is no order in the universe anymore. The divorce rate is skyrocketing daily; libertarianism reigns, and children no longer seem to place faith in the family unit. They think it is safer to live alone. God help us!

If children decide to run away from home, they discover it is different in the streets, especially in large cities of America. Then loneliness closes in, followed by disappointment and depression. Finally, they feel ashamed and too embarrassed to return home. Most runaways end up in the hands of pimps, drug lords or both. Some enter the world of prostitution, dance in strip clubs, or kill themselves. Suicide is not the answer. Parents, please pay attention regardless of what your child or children has done, always keep an open heart, open door, and an open home and the lights on for them.

People that are lonely can also become conscious of wanting too much attention. They lack attention and when they do get it, it seems like it is not enough. Those that are blind, deaf, bound in wheelchairs, elderly or bed ridden and chronically ill usually have this need. Because they do not acquire the attention that they crave, remorse and bitterness sets in. They also become withdrawn.

Most lonely people hardly take the initiative to go out, or meet anyone, or participate in anything. They often become introverts; they keep everything bottled up inside of them, and this can be detrimental to the human mind.

It often results in serious mental problems. This is the main reason why psychiatrists probe into their patients' mind, asking questions for long periods of time. This helps to determine if they can be of some assistance to the patient.

Also, there are some lonely people who travel from country to country, striving to alleviate their loneliness. They travel by car, ship or by plane in their quest to cure their problem. In their travels, they attempt to meet new people, experiment with new partners, new ideas, toying with the idea that it would help them. To some extent this might help, but they usually return home with a cloud of loneliness hanging over their heads.

It is noted that homemakers (wives at home) suffer from loneliness constantly and daily. A certain wife confessed, "When my husband is gone for the day, I am all alone. The children are in school I do not know what to do with myself. I have a beautiful home, nice surroundings, good neighbors, a car to drive, money to spend, but believe me when I tell you my home feels like a jail sometimes. Worst of all, the emptiness I feel inside plus an empty home is a killer."

Most unfaithfulness in marriage occurs when either party is away from the other and of course, alone. Most unfaithfulness frequently occurs among wives who are at home alone. As a minister I speak and counsel people from week to week. On one such occasion, I spoke to a certain lady she confided in me and said, "I know that I am embarrassingly overweight, but the loneliness I go through makes it seem like I cannot stop eating. I eat constantly and do not know how to control myself. Not surprisingly, loneliness affects a vast majority of the population who eats and cannot control themselves. Other eating disorders including anorexia and bulimia also stem from loneliness.

Television has become one of the most powerful tools of communication in these modern times. The sad thing about watching TV is that you cannot talk back. Christian television can be of some spiritual benefit but most of cable, satellite, network TV, is filled with violence, filthy language, murder, crimes. According to a recent report, seventy percent of the population watches an average of thirty-five hours of television Monday through Friday, and twenty-five hours on Saturday and Sunday. That is sixty hours of television for the week. Out of seventy percent, forty percent are glued to the television day and night.

Early in the morning on one occasion, I saw a certain man standing by himself. I approached him and the smell of whiskey was very strong on his breath. I asked him why he drank whiskey and he bluntly answered, "I am very lonely." Consuming alcohol was his way of alleviating his feeling of loneliness. I could not just walk away from this man without explaining to him the reason why he drank the way he did: he was searching for peace, real joy and happiness, he said I need to be myself again I am looking for wholeness and healing in my life. I took time with him and explained the dangers and the results of alcoholic drinks, and he listened. More importantly, I ministered to him about the love of Jesus. His life was different from then on.

It has been reported and surprisingly so, to certain extent alcoholism is sweeping this country. Teenagers and young people in general are the victims of whiskey, beer, and other alcoholic drinks. As a whole, people of all ages are developing into alcoholics, aiming to drown their loneliness and other problems they are experiencing.

A fine-looking lady named Stacy asked me to pray for her. However, before praying for her, I noticed her cracked and swollen lips coupled with the strong smell of cigarettes emitting from her breath. I asked her what she wanted me to pray about. She confided that she smoked two to three packs of cigarettes a day and consumed one beer after another. I asked her why she did it and she replied, "I'm so lonely. In my search to alleviate my loneliness, I tried cigarettes and beer, but believe me, it seems like I am going around in circles. Nothing satisfies me, and I hope there is an answer somewhere." I prayed with her as she wept, after which she confessed how God and prayer made a difference in her life.

Pornography is a multi-billion-dollar business in this country. It too, attracts people who are lonely. It destroys the fabric of a person, especially when that person is lonely. Pornography is displayed in every convenience store. Adult bookstores have sprung up everywhere, seemingly overnight, and to add insult to injury, via satellite and the Internet, all types of sexual activities and porn shows can be channeled right into people's homes. What does this have to do with loneliness? Here is the story of a young man, whose name is withheld as he confided in me for counsel and help. This young man went to a larger city to work and better himself.

When he arrived in this particular city, he rented a certain motel that offered weekly rates, which was convenient for him. As he relayed the incident to me, he said, "Pastor, after I settled in the motel and started flipping through the channels. To my amazement and shock, I discovered a channel with every type of pornography and sexual act." In his heart, he knew he should have disconnected that particular channel or checked out of the motel, but he said that he was lonely. He continued to watch the program and one night of looking at pornography led to another, then to weeks and months of viewing.

As you can imagine, it became hard for him to concentrate. The pornography affected his mind and being deprived of good company, relatives and friends, he found himself entangled in a web of ungodly, unholy relationships. He said, "I was so lonely that I allowed this filth to get into my mind, my system, and it drove me to do things that I did not have control over." After a long period of counseling and prayer with me, he was finally free from the bondage of pornography. When lonely, one's imagination runs wild. A person's thought life can become out of control, sometimes suggesting that person to do things that he or she normally would not do.

Truck drivers are some of the loneliest people. While traveling to one of my revival meetings, I stopped at a truck stop to fill my car with gas, rest a little and eat. While eating a sandwich a truck driver who somehow figured I was a minister introduced himself to me, we spoke for a while as he confided and spoke to me, "he said when he is away from home, his wife and children, he just cannot handle the loneliness he faces while on the highways of America".

Worst of all, he said "his mind becomes obsessed with the thought that his wife is unfaithful to him; that his children do not really love him. Furthermore, he said that when he is home, he does not think or feel that way. These thoughts were originating from him being lonely; I spoke to him for a while and prayed with him, he confessed feeling so much better.

Recently there was a report on television, which was even published in a leading newspaper. According to the report dozens and dozens of people commit suicide annually by jumping off a certain bridge. The report stated that guards were being placing on that bridge to stop the flow of people who go there with the intent of jumping off the bridge to commit suicide, their reasons, the pressures of life, lack of family and friends, financial problems, or some social related problem.

Some of these people were caught in time and their lives spared. When asked why they attempted suicide, they did not hesitate to mention that they were lonely.

Suicide is not the answer to loneliness. More Americans now die of suicide than from car accidents, according to the Centers for Disease Control and Prevention, a disturbing statistic that some experts say points to the true depths of the US economic crisis.

From 1999 to 2010, the suicide rate among US citizens between the ages of 35-64 rose about 30 per cent, to 17.6 deaths per 100,000 people, a jump from 13.7. In 2010 there 38, 364 suicides, there are more suicides among middle-aged men and women. Among the male population, the greatest increases were among those aged 50–54 years and 55–59 years, (49.4 per cent, from 20.6 to 30.7, and 47.8 per cent, from 20.3 to 30.0 respectively). Among females, suicide rates tended to increase with age. The largest percentage increase in suicide rate was observed among women aged 60–64 years (59.7 per cent, from 4.4 to 7.0).Suicide rates from 1999 to 2010 "increased significantly" across all four geographic areas and in 39 states. The state of Wyoming recorded the highest increase in suicides with a 78.8 per cent jump (31.1 per 100,000), while even the sunny state of Hawaii witnessed a 61.2 per cent increase (21.9 per 100,000). As shocking as the newly released data on US suicide rates are, many believe the numbers are too low since many deaths are not treated as actual suicides. Why all these suicides?

Of these figures above most of these suicidal were related to loneliness. Suicide is not the way out, according to the Bible God's word, God is the author of life and He alone has the power to give and take life. Suicide is a sin, for it is taking a human life, it is self inflicted murder. The Bible which is God's word clearly expresses the sanctity of human life. God is the author of life and He alone has the power to give and take a life. Here are two Biblical references which God states are against an individual taking their own life or committing suicide, taking one's life does not guarantee a Godly eternity. *Exodus 20:13, Job 1:21.*

The previous chapter dealt with the apparent natural causes of loneliness. In the following chapter, you will discover the root cause of this diabolical, complicated, "Dr. Jekyll and Mr. Hyde" sickness called loneliness.

CHAPTER SEVEN:
WHO ARE THE LONELY PEOPLE

Lonely people inhabit every nation under the sun. This diabolical, complicated, "Dr. Jekyll and Mr. Hyde" sickness affects people of every race, color, and creed. This disease spans to include multi-millionaires, millionaires, rich, middle class, and the poor.

A certain multi-billionaire who controlled large industries, possessed several jets, had a wonderful family, thousands of friends, and could have bought anything money could buy, isolated himself in a hotel room for a long period of time. He refused to see anyone. After some years he died in his filth, naked, surrounded by raggedy clothes, empty bottles, and torn up newspapers.

The room was infested with roaches and rats. Why couldn't all the money, prestige, and fame keep him happy? Even though he had everything, his life was empty and lonely. That is what drove him to an untimely death. The physiological problem of loneliness spares no one regardless of his or her position in life, lofty or noble, humble, peasant, rich or poor. It was stated that movie stars who entertain the masses are some of the loneliest people in the world. They might look good on camera for movies and television but inwardly, most of them are extremely lonely.

Highly paid professional athletes and coaches suffer from loneliness as well. Lonely people emerge from every walk of life and profession. Lonely people cross your path every day. You travel with them. You work with them. You eat with them. You even live in the same home with some of them. You see lonely people in planes, trains, buses, cars, and taxis commuting like everyone else. They work in offices, businesses, and stores. They shop like everyone else. Some of them even have a smile on their face but behind that happy persona is a lonely individual.

Some of the loneliest people in the world are truck drivers. You can look at them and see that faraway look of loneliness in their eyes. I have spoken to some of them; believe me; many of them do have a home but they are away most of the time and can hardly enjoy their family and homes.

To no great surprise, lonely people exist in hospitals, nursing homes, and mental institutions. As well, prisons and public jails are predominately filled with extremely lonely inmates. Motel and hotel rooms, the stadiums and ballparks are full of lonely people.

Why do you think some of them attend ballgames? I never go to ballgames, but just to spend time with one of my sons, I went to a ballgame with him. While there, I spoke to a young man sitting next to me who was enthusiastically enjoying the game. In the midst of our conversation, he found out I was a minister and said to me, "I do not know where I am going after this game" I just hate going back to that old, rented room to be alone."

Loneliness strikes most people whose calling, and profession takes them away from home months and even years at a time. In my research, I was shocked to discover that the highest percentage of men and women that are lonely are MARRIED people. This accounts for the high divorce rate in America, Canada, Europe, the Orient and other parts of the world.

After a large crusade in one of the Islands, I went to the airport to check in and fly back to Miami. While checking in, it was discovered that there was a mistake on my ticket, realizing their mistake the airline promoted me from coach to first class. After the flight took off, there was a well-dressed gentleman sitting adjacent to my seat and we struck up a conversation and I discovered I was speaking to the president of a large company. I could tell by his approach to me that he was longing to talk to someone. In the midst of our conversation, he blurted out, "People do not realize what I go through. I spend thousands of hours by myself; two or three weeks out of every month I travel for business and rarely see or spend time with my family.

"He blurted out, "I cannot handle this loneliness anymore". Thank God for this businessman, I was about to make a decision for the title of this book, he certainly helped confirmed the title of this book.

Don't let appearances fool you. People live in beautiful homes; some of them have smiles on their faces, dress fancy, possess pretty cars, have money in the bank and prestige. Money is not a concern to them; they could purchase anything money could buy. However, loneliness looms over them. Some of these very same people are very lonely.

And what of the middle-class citizens? They do everything possible to make a living. Many holds two jobs (and in some instances three jobs.) Often the arrangement goes like this: the wife comes in from a 9-5 job and the husband goes out to his night job. It's becoming increasingly common for both spouses to have a full-time and a part-time job especially at this present time with the economy waning daily. Americans are in deep steep financial problems as they are forced to work, day and night just to make extra money to pay their mortgage, car, credit cards and for the bare necessities.

Evidently, this has caused husbands, wives, families to be separated from each other, which is causing to many inconveniences and loneliness. It is said that during this time there has been untold amount of separation and divorces. Thousands of children are alone at home, school, or somewhere else, but all, children included, confess that they fight loneliness each day because of the pressures of daily living and parents working.

While reading this book if you are faced with this type of situation, it will not hurt to when the moment arises, take some time with your wife, husband, child or children and kin folks this will help.

As a minister, I often travel to foreign countries. After leaving the airport, I travel to areas where our crusades are held. I have often stood before crowds of approximately 400,000 (sometimes more, sometimes less), participating in meetings that usually last a week. I like to visit some remote areas of some these countries. I like visiting the inhabitants of the poorest towns and villages of these countries. I've visited and ministered to people whose dwelling places are shanty shacks made of coconut leaves or mud huts, and even though I do my best to help these people with food and clothing, what really captivates my attention is the look of loneliness on their faces. You will not realize the joy that reflects on their faces when someone like me goes to visit, minister and help them.

New York City! Manhattan! Times Square! Broadway! The name of this city rings a bell to all Americans. In my travels I have been to New York literally hundreds of times. Believe me when I tell you it is an exciting city with all of its high-rise buildings, ritzy lights, and towering bridges that connect with other cities such as the Bronx, Brooklyn, New Jersey etc. The fast-paced subway trains, buses, taxicabs, limos, and private cars all jostle to their destination, some trying to outdo each other, transporting their passengers to and fro to their various destinations.

Whenever I am in "The Big Apple," as it is affectionately referred to, I anticipate the approaching nightfall. At night, as all the lights are turned on both on the inside and outside of the high skyscrapers, I deliberately gaze on its multi-cultural population of people as I walk the streets of New York City. I inhale the scent of the foods of different cultures cooking in the restaurants adjacent to the sidewalks and take in the sights and sounds of many nationalities all clustered within a few city blocks.

What really catches my attention in the crowds of thousands of people that walk its streets at night? It is the look of loneliness on their faces. Ask these people what their biggest problem is and most of them would tell you as they told me, "Its loneliness." All the sights, sounds, and culture of the most amazing city in the world are powerless to conquer the disease of loneliness.

PART 2
OVERCOMING LONELINESS
CHAPTER EIGHT
YOU CANNOT UNSCRAMBLE EGGS

You can pull yourself out of situations! But try as hard as you can there are some things you personally cannot undo. The mistakes people have made in the past can haunt them for the rest of their lives, if they allow them to. Now that you have the courage and strength to go on, and because of will power and determination, you might try your best to put everything back together. There's no harm in trying but without success, some things you did in the past, faults failures, mistakes you've made have caused everything to be in shambles and scrambled also bits and pieces are here there and everywhere.

It is a fact that no one could unscramble and an egg, personally speaking yours truly have had to fix breakfast many times, I would heat up the oil or butter then put the eggs in the skillet with the intention of cooking them over easy, but it was not beginning to turn out and cook like I wanted it to. Guess what? I had to scramble them. In no way I could unscramble these eggs after its done scrambled. Just a sense of humor here, if eggs are good poach them, if they are slightly addled cook them over easy, if eggs are no good, scramble them. This is where some people might be, in   their situations, problems and loneliness.

Have you ever heard of the statement "You cannot unscramble eggs" the things that you have done in the past possibly has reached to the point of already being divorced, children might be no where to be found, business went down, perhaps you lost your job and you and everything went downhill. Loneliness depression, oppression has had you in a tailspin and you do not know where you at, but you must be reminded that God is the only one who has the power to deliver you and put the pieces back together again.

Where do you go for help? You need somebody to help you. God uses people, but God is the only one that can help. God alone can unscramble eggs or put things back together. Whatever idea you might have of God, I would like you to understand that He is not in the big blue yonder waiting with a sledgehammer to bop anyone on their head or to strike someone dead. Whenever someone makes mistake or do wrong, God does not want to punish you and send you to hell. By the way God does not send anyone to hell; the choice you make causes you to go there. Hell wasn't even created for men and women, *Matt. 25:41* Yes! God is a God of judgment when deserving. But generally, God is a God of mercy, grace and of course love. He cares for everyone and believe me, there was no greater love shown to mankind that that was shown when He sent His Son Jesus Christ to die on the cross, for everything that you are going through. Your problems, needs, circumstances and situations are not impossible to God

Your present situation might be very frustrating, but your end can be your beginning. This can be done by reaching out to someone that is greater and bigger than you. God uses people but there some situations and problems that no human can help, and this is where God comes in if people will allow him.

To help you understand God, I would like to borrow a thought that I heard while traveling, on one of Billy Graham's Sunday evening broadcasts. He said that once his and him was walking through the woods. His son was a little boy at the time and of course shorter than his father. The son saw his father stepped on an ant bed, hundreds of them came crawling out of the ant bed, some of them were killed and some were hurt, then his son said to his father "Daddy can you help those ants"? Billy Graham said to his son, "Son for me to help those ants I have to become like one of them.

This is exactly what God did for us; He became like one of us, by sending His Son, Jesus Christ to live among us and die for mankind. Jesus was born like any one of us, and then He grew up like all humans do. He knows what it is like to be human, to be hungry, thirsty, tired and weary, tempted, tried, and tested. He had natural needs like us. He also knew what it felt like to be lonely and forsaken. The Bible tells us that there is not a problem you encounter, that God does not understand.

What else do us humans wants God to do than what He has already done. When God sent Jesus Christ to die on the Cross this was God's way of saying to us, I love and care for you. Jesus lasts few words before He died on the Cross recorded in the Gospel of *John 19:30,* "*It is finished"* these words meant that every problem including loneliness was paid for by Jesus dying on the Cross, all an individual has to do is reach out to God and call on Him for help.

This book is written in a manner so that saint and sinner alike can understand. Some of you reading this book might have never read a Bible in your life, but here is a Scripture referring to the death of Jesus Christ on the Cross and Hs resurrection. If you not mind read and meditate:

> *"For we have not an high priest which cannot be*
> *touched with the feeling of our infirmities; but was in all*
> *points tempted like as we are, yet without sin. Let us therefore*
> *come boldly unto the throne of grace, that we may obtain*
> *mercy, and find grace to help in time of need." KJV Hebrews*
> *4:15-16.*

Stop wondering, worrying of how everything is going to come back together again. Worries cause sleepless nights, wrinkled faces, zombie like statues and heart attacks. Most everyone has a heard of an old colloquial statement, why worry when you can pray. Yours truly whenever ministering says it the other way around "why pray when you could worry" which means to say some people do more worrying instead of praying. Jesus spoke some words in the Bible recorded in the Gospel of *Luke 18:1-8,* He made reference of a widow woman who has an enemy that was giving her a rough time and she went to a judge of that land once and asks him to stop her enemy. But the judge did not help her. Did she give up? No! She kept bothering the judge day after day week after week; finally, the judge gave in and rewarded her by stopping this woman's adversary or enemy. How did Jesus conclude this illustration of this woman? "WHEN, THE SON OF MAN COMETH, SHALL HE FAITH ON EARTH".

Why did Jesus make this statement? (1) He used this illustration two thousand years ago, to inspire us of today regardless of the situation you're in, don't give up until you get the victory. This also means regardless of the mistakes you have made in the past. (2) In the last days there will be so much pressure, problems, pining, grumbling, complaining, mourning, groaning griping, fussing, swearing, cussing! Jesus is also telling us that in the last days there will be all types of problems, wars, earthquakes, famine, pestilences, sicknesses, diseases, betrayal, depression, oppression and loneliness. Jesus looks through the corridors of time and seeing all of these things happening, He meant, would anyone living on earth would have faith in God. Please remember FAITH IN GOD IS THE ONLY THING THAT CAN CAUSE YOU TO SURVIVE.

You might ask, "How do I or anyone else unscramble eggs FAITH IN GOD. Someone might ask. How do I begin to have faith in God, everyone has faith in someone or something, but real faith begins with the BORN-AGAIN EXPERIENCE? This is not a book on faith neither it is about the born-again experience. But if the reader, especially those who suffer from loneliness and all other related problems can be helped, faith in God is very important. The Born-again experience initiates your relationship with God as the faith life and a relationship with God begins. Anyone who chooses to understand more about the Born-Again experience begins a faith walk with God. Please read the Bible the Gospel of *John 3 and the book of Hebrews 11.*

Faith is the connection between you and God; faith believes God can do all things. My definition of faith is "believing God to do what He said He will do." You cannot and will not develop faith by listening to the negative things that certain people say; faith comes by reading and studying the Bible, the Word of God.

God's Promises:

What did God promise to do, and where do you locate His promises? You will find them on the dusty Bible lying on the coffee table or on your bookshelf. Perhaps your grandmother or mother gave you a Bible, if you are in a hotel room; chances are there's a Bible in the drawer. There are even free online Bible programs. Bible Gateway is one such program (www.biblegateway.com).

All of God's promises are found in the Bible; just pick up and begin to read what's in it, especially the Psalms and the Gospels. As you begin to read, you will discover what God promised to do. As you read you will want to read more of it. Consistent reading will begin to build faith in your heart to believe God to work in your life and situation. I recall watching a little girl trying to put a puzzle together; no matter how she tried, she could not do it. Finally, in frustration she broke down and started crying, she ran to her mother and cried, "Mama, would you please help me fix it?"

The mother came over and put the puzzle back together. The mother asked, "See how easy it is?" "Yes," said the little girl, "but I need somebody bigger than me to help me." Who is that? somebody bigger than you? HE IS GOD. Yes, help from another human being is essential and expected, but who is bigger than God? He made you; He knows your situation better more than anyone else. This is the reason you must turn to God and trust Him. Never get to the point where you feel you can exist or go through life without God.

God made us He gave our parents the ability to pro-create; every part of you was through the miracle of birth and growth. The very fact that you are breathing at this moment, what would happen if you should suddenly loose your breath! You will be dead. Just thank Him that you are alive and well, you might think, "Well, look what I have accomplished. I am well off; I have a nice home, a wonderful family, money in the bank, nice cars, and no financial worries." To some of you reading this book this might not be your situation. Life as per say seem like it's against you in every way, you might be struggling to make ends meet, but having an attitude that everything even God is against you, this attitude will not help. But learn to thank, worship and praise God in spite of all the adversities you are going through.

Generally speaking, weather, you are poor, middle class or rich, ask yourself this question: what if you are suddenly struck with a heart attack, cancer, AIDS or financial ruin? What happens then? So many people die daily, and some lose it all in so many different ways, but the greatest feeling is to know there is a God and He wants to help us in spite of our failures.

Before, I quote the words of a man that had everything. I am not referring to just an ordinary man, but a king. King David had insurmountable complex and various conflicting problems: the responsibility to govern a nation of millions of people, handling the daily problems of governing a people, dealing with the threats of Israel enemies on every side, there were times he had to lead his Army in war, there were disloyal generals, leaders who turned their backs on him, sons and daughters who did not walk in the ways of God. Most of all he had to deal with the mistake he made in his early life. But what and who kept King David of the Bible, Faith in God and of course God. Here are some words he prayed when faced with distress and loneliness:

Hear my prayer, O LORD, and let my cry come unto thee. Hide not thy face from me in the day when I am in trouble; incline thine ear unto me: in the day when I call answer me speedily.

For my days are consumed like smoke, and my bones are burned as an hearth. My heart is smitten, and withered like grass; so that I forget to eat my bread.

By reason of the voice of my groaning my bones cleave to my skin. I am like a pelican of the wilderness: I am like an owl of the desert. I watch, and am as a sparrow alone upon the house top. (loneliness)

Mine enemies reproach me all the day; and they that are mad against me are sworn against me."

My days are like a shadow that declineth; and I am withered like grass. But thou, O LORD, shall endure for ever; and thy remembrance unto all generations."

"He will regard the prayer of the destitute, and not despise their prayer." Psalm 102:1-8, 11, 12, 17

CHAPTER NINE:
WHICH WAY IS UP?

There was a time in this country when some people, especially Hollywood actors, did not believe there was a devil. But someone in Hollywood made a movie called *The Exorcist* and then more people realized that demons and evil spirits existed. Satanism, voodoo, witchcraft, and the occult is luring millions of people, while the religion of the East is making more inroads into the hearts of the people of the U.S. The war in Iraq (even though our troops has been withdrawn) is still the center of controversy, however, people must realize that Jesus spoke about wars and rumors of wars that would occur in our time. War is prophecy being fulfilled pointing to the not too distant Second Return of Jesus Christ.

And as he sat upon the mount of Olives, the disciples came unto him privately, saying,

Tell us, when shall these things be? And what shall be the sign of thy coming, and of the end of the world?

And Jesus answered and said unto them, Take heed that no man deceive you. For many shall come in my name, saying, I am Christ; and shall deceive many.

And ye shall hear of wars and rumors of wars: see that ye be not troubled: for all these things must come to pass, but the end is not yet.

For nation shall rise against nation, and kingdom against kingdom: and there shall be famines, and pestilences, and earthquakes, in divers' places. All these are the beginning of sorrows." Matthew 24:3-8

Every phase of our society, including heads of government, is being mesmerized by constant scandals. The future is uncertain, over the past years we have seen more militant organizations rise up in this country and outside interferences that resulted in the Twin Towers in New York came down, series of bombings, murder is on the rise, crime is on the increase, drug use and alcohol consumption is taking its toll on millions of young people and adults, children are disappearing from homes, and some of them are being abused more than ever before. Television shows are becoming more vulgar, while the devil is influencing certain people to rid the airways of Christian TV and wholesome Christian Programs.

Most of our schools do not want anything to do with prayer and the Bible, and students and people are walking in with guns and knives, killing teachers and students. One out of five marriages ends in divorce, and families are torn apart. In spite of modern scientific breakthroughs in the medical field, AIDS is already taking its toll on thousands upon thousands of victims. More "new" sicknesses and diseases are popping up, plus millions of people are complaining of stress. It goes without saying that this type of lifestyle leads to fear and of course, loneliness. With all of these things going on, intense battles are being raged in the hearts and minds of many people; it seems as though every person you meet is going through some kind of crisis

Some one might say I thought this was a book pertaining to loneliness and its results, but the author wants to bring you to a point of realization, because of the turmoil that is pervasive and occurring outside, inside and within the hearts and minds of everyone. The adverse effects of all this are taking place here in America and the World, these situations have place severe pressures on the populace worldwide. This has caused millions of men, women, young people and children to be forced into some types of seclusion which has caused millions to be driven into a life of loneliness. But there is a way out and the way out is by **looking up**.

I remember so vividly at a certain time of my life and ministry, I was going through a crisis while at home in Georgia. During this time, I decided to take a drive on one of the quiet, out-of-the-way country roads close to where I live. I kept on driving and driving and the further I drove I noticed that the pine trees were very tall and high, taller and higher than all the pine trees I had ever seen in that area. I stopped without any inclination as to why I was stopping I got out of the car and walked, prayed and meditated for a while. While meditating, I heard the Spirit of God spoke to me He said, "Look at that pine tree." Immediately I lifted up my eyes and in the midst of all the pines I saw one of the tallest and most beautiful pine trees I had ever seen. This made me curious, and I wondered what God was trying to show and say to me.

I kept looking and looking at this soaring pine tree, and then I heard the Spirit of God spoke to me again and said, "What is that pine tree doing?" I continued staring for quite a while then it dawned on me that this pine tree was pointing upwards, seemingly looking upwards.

God, I prayed you are trying to tell me something, at the moment I heard the still voice of God saying to me, just as that pine tree is pointing and looking upwards, look upwards look to God.

Someone might ask, is it possible for God to speak to a person like He did to me? Yes, He wants to speak to us all the time, even in crisis and loneliness, but we need to take time to stop and listen to what God wants to say to us. God speaks by revelation, visions and dreams. He also speaks especially through the Word of God the Bible, He speaks in many ways but last but not least God speaks by a still small voice; however, when He speaks, He wants to bring us closer to Him. God showed to me to think back to the time when this tallest of pine was just a seed; it was alone in the ground covered with dirt and it could not be seen. But it started to grow and from the moment it sprung up from the ground, it kept pointing or looking upwards. While it was growing seasons changed, there were times it was so cold, but it kept pointing upwards; there were times it was so hot, but it kept pointing or looking upwards.

No one paid it any attention, but it continued pointing upwards and continued to grow. In times of fire, it kept pointing upwards. Perhaps while it was a tiny tree, people stepped on it, but it kept pointing upwards. Times of rain, winds, and storms came, but it kept pointing upwards and growing until it became one of the tallest pine trees. This pine was majestically grown and still pointing upwards".

One of the major problems facing America today, as well as other countries, is that people are looking to everyone and everything else except God for solutions. Some look to actors and actresses, sports personalities, entertainers, politicians and television show hosts. Within the religious world, many look to television ministers (some of them do help people) but remember that no matter whom they are, they are fallible; some of them will disappoint you but God will never let you down. Honestly, sometimes God seems far away but He will answer prayer and come through for anyone who looks and trust in Him.

Human beings have a tendency of looking to other human beings, is this wrong? No! There are people who are qualified who has the ability and knowledge of helping people in their situation, problems, circumstances and of course loneliness. But most of the time there are people who suffer from chronic loneliness cannot be helped by professionals but looking upwards and trusting God will not hurt but help.

Your idea of God might be very vague, but I know beyond a shadow of a doubt that God is real! I will never forget especially at the age of fourteen - fifteen even though I grew up in church. The loneliness I experienced was like an excruciating pain combined with fear and a void within my spirit, the emptiness that I felt within me, most of all going to eternity without God. This feeling haunted me night and day. With all of this going on within my mind and spirit I began searching for answers and help in the quagmire of religions, denominations, organizations, philosophy, and mysticism. In the midst of an era of philosophy and spiritual confusion, everyone was telling me that they were right. Most of them were like inept physicians void of value and cures. Then I started looking upwards to God. He came to me, saved and delivered me.

I did not begin a relationship with God in some church meeting (although one could). He came into my heart when I knelt down on my knees in a little room and I prayed to Him like He was standing right close to me "God, I know you are real and all that the Bible says that you are: I thank you for sending Jesus Christ to die on the Cross for all of my sins, sickness, problems, and trouble, I ask you Jesus to come into my heart and save me from all my sins, give me peace, joy, real happiness and contentment, fill my heart with your presence, take away the emptiness and loneliness that I have been feeling: Help me God as I wept I looked up, He came down: The moment I did this, I felt the Spirit of God came into my spirit and fill my entire being with His presence. From that moment to this present time, I have had such a wonderful experience of peace, joy, satisfaction, and real happiness, most of all, the emptiness and loneliness that I had inside of me disappeared.

The reason for this when there were no one in sight then I began looking upwards and He came down, looking up can be just looking up, but look up to God with a desire that He would come down to help you or anyone that is in need of help, and He will.

These are words of the King David from the Bible,

"I will lift up mine eyes unto the hills, from whence
cometh my help. My help cometh from the LORD, which
made heaven and earth.

He will not suffer thy foot to be
moved: he that keepeth thee will not slumber. Behold, he
that keepeth Israel shall neither slumber nor sleep.

The LORDis thy keeper: the LORD is thy shade upon thy right hand. The
sun shall not smite thee by day, nor the moon by night.

The LORD shall preserve thee from all evil: he shall
preserve thy soul. The LORD shall preserve thy going out
and thy coming in from this time forth, and even for evermore.
Psalm 23.

What was the psalmist referring to? Was it just the hills he was speaking about to look to? No, he was referring to looking beyond the hills and up to God, the King of kings and Lord of lords. Each time the psalmist looked at the hills, he remembered how GOD brought his forefathers out from the land of Egypt, with miracles, signs, and wonders. Whenever he looked towards the hills, he saw the glory of God. He saw God as "El Gibor," the great and mighty One who is able to deliver in every situation, who is able to solve any problem, and meet each or every need, even loneliness.

Your inward look depends on your outlook; your outlook depends on your upward look. One of the prophets in the Bible, the prophet Isaiah became so tired of all that was going on around him. The Nation of Israel had turned their back on God, and Isaiah was frustrated and felt helpless in this situation. In his earlier life depended so much on his uncle Uzziah who was the King of Israel but when King Uzziah died, Isaiah became very distraught, worried, and lonely. Nonetheless, during this time of crisis, he encountered one of the greatest experiences with God.

On a certain day Isaiah was in prayer, he looked up and saw Jesus, and it forever changed his life. If you are looking for help from certain people and material things, you are being deceived. Such pursuits are vague and only last for a short while. Times of crises are times that you hurt, feel disappointed, and let down. Most of all during such times discouragement sets in. But in times of crisis, you can experience the greatest victory in your life and encounter an experience with God...if you would only look up.

Eagles, one of the most interesting studies are the life and ways of an eagle. An eagle is one of the birds that God created which is spoken of as extra ordinary. Eagles are admired the world over as living symbols of power, freedom, and transcending. There are more than sixty species of Eagle. Eagles are different from many other birds of prey mainly by their size, more powerfully build and heavier head and beak. Most eagles are larger than raptors and vultures. Eagles have unusual eyes with very large pupils, the amazing thing about an eagle's eyes, they contain a million light sensitive cells per square millimeter of retina, five times more than a human two hundred thousand. While human's see three basic colors an eagle sees five.

The eagle's vision is one of the sharpest among birds and animals and can spot a rabbit up to, two or three miles away. Eagles soar to new heights by using currents of air; they will spread their wings and feathers of their tails to carry them to new heights, they used contrary winds to their advantage not to work against them, they discern which way the winds are blowing and use the winds to soar and carry them higher. Flying with the winds saves an eagle strength and energy because it does not have to flap its wings.

Loneliness and all other problems can use as a steppingstone to mount up like eagles and not be caught in the raging storms of life. Why this brief lesson about an eagle, the entire Bible is filled with references concerning this majestic bird, there is a reason why the eagle is mentioned about sixty times or more in the Word of God. God never meant for you to spend the balance of your life being lonely, stop listening to the people who tells you, your life was meant to be this way. No matter what the problems, even if lonely, but if you will look up and of course look up to God He will help.

Here we are in the year of 2014, with all the technology, wisdom, knowledge, industries, medical breakthrough, inventions, and more, some people have given the idea that they do not need God. And this is the reason the human race is in total disarray, disappointment and degradation. Human beings are at a point they can hardly cope with the problems of everyday life. This is the reason we have so much of spiritual confusion, diseases, sicknesses, crimes, corruption, mental and social problems, combine with nervous breakdowns and loneliness.

But there is a secret, thank God thousands are beginning to feel the need of Divine help and are turning to God for support and strength. I never thought I would see the day and the time when some of the news media are writing and posting articles on the internet and other wise, that going to Church and prayer helps. Mentioned was made of the fact that the people who goes to church and pray suffer less stress. Jesus spoke these words two thousand years ago and all and individual has to do is read what Jesus said in *Matthew 11:28, come unto me all ye labor and are heavy laden and I will give you rest, take my yoke upon you for my burden is light and my yoke is easy.*

Here is one of the most powerful verses in the Bible, God speaking through the Prophet *Isaiah 40:1-7, KJV.*

To whom then will ye liken me, or shall I be equal? Saith the Holy one,

Lift up your eyes on high, and behold who hath created these things, that bringeth out their host by number: he calleth them all by names by the greatness of his might, for that he is strong in power; not one faileth.

Why sayest thou, O Jacob, and speakest, O Israel, My way is hid from the LORD, and my judgment is passed over from my God?

Hast thou not known? hast thou not heard that the everlasting God, the LORD, the Creator of the ends of the earth, faintest not, neither is weary? there is no searching of his understanding. He giveth power to the faint; and to them that have no might he increaseth strength.

Even the youths shall faint and be weary, and the young men shall utterly fall: But they that wait upon the LORD shall renew their strength; they shall mount up with wings as eagles; they shall run, and not be weary; and they shall walk, and not faint.

Note: The word" *mount up"* is proceeded by the words *"they that wait upon then Lord"* being successful in life, your desires granted (not fleshly lust) realizing your dreams and accomplishments, depends on waiting on God. This does not mean that an individual must sit down and do nothing. There are thousands of lonely people who just sit down and do nothing, this attitude plunges them into deep depression and oppression.

There are some people with the attitude that God is obligated to them, no he made us we are obligated to Him. But here is the key to anything that pertains to life and God's blessing *"they that wait upon the Lord"* an individual must be willing to recognize and come to God before he blesses them.

This true to life story sums up this chapter. A millionaire who went into a restaurant ordered steak, mashed potato, gravy, with sides of corn, greens beans and rolls. At the same time an ordinary everyday hard-working man came in the same restaurant and ordered about the same meal. This millionaire could barely touch or eat his meal. He was suffering from heart problems, indigestion, ulcers, etc, (this is not always the case of all rich people) looked at this man who lifted up his head and thank God for the meal that was set before him. Then this same man ate every bit of food from his plate. Then the millionaire told the waitress "I wish I could eat all my food like that man". What made the difference? The millionaire noticed this other man lifted up his head and thank God for the meal before eating. Always look which way is up, God.

CHAPTER TEN:
"YOU" CAN PULL "YOURSELF" OUT

You are down in the dumps, oppressed, depressed, mixed up and confused, and do not know what next to do or which way to go. You are and locked out, locked in and locked down, shut in and shut out, cold in the winter and all year long, and most of all, lonely. Last night's rendezvous and party of frolicking, booze, and dance has given you one of the worst hangovers you ever had. Early in the day you have smoked several packs of cigarettes and guzzled a few cans of beer. As you think about drinking another one, you wonder if you should drink it; you hesitate because it seems like it's doing nothing for you (and it's not). You drink it, because your system craves for more of it.

You cannot control yourself or your habits: the crack, cocaine, marijuana and alcohol and more. Deep down inside of you something tells you that you cannot go on like this. You watch one television show after another, yet you are not satisfied. You get dressed and run down to the video store to rent some of the latest movies. You sit there and watch scene after scene, viewing all the murder, nudity, filth, cursing, sex and violence. You think about your own lifestyle; the illicit sex and sex partners you have been involved with, both in and out of marriage, has suddenly become meaningless and the fear of Aids or some other STD is gnawing inside of you, the marriage vows you repeated or spoke at the church alter in the presence of God meant nothing to you, your marriage did not last and now you are contemplating divorce.

Perhaps your spouse has walked out on you; and what you wanted was to reach the goal of the American dream, has turned into the American nightmare. And now you are lonely and in despair. The sad thing about it is that the psychiatrist, doctors, attorneys, pills, voodoo, witchcraft, trips, vacations, Ouija board yoga, meditation and all the religions and solutions have tried has not given you any real satisfaction or peace of mind or help in your loneliness. There is still that aggravating feeling of emptiness and loneliness deep inside of you. At this point you are the only person who can pull yourself out of the situations you got yourself in. In an earlier chapter "you cannot unscramble eggs" mentioned was made you have to reach out to someone; the emphasis was to reach out for professional help and FAITH IN GOD. All else can help, but God is the only one that can help and deliver you from all problems and in particular loneliness. But at this particular chapter it must be emphasized that "you" are the key person if you are going to be set from any problem or problems, especially if you are lonely. If an individual is desperate enough and willing to be free, but there is a key and the key for your salvation and deliverance now, are YOU.

Several years ago, a young man whose life correlates with some of the things mentioned above, made an appointment and went to see a prominent minister in the city where he lived, with the intention of getting some help. The minister graciously invited the young man into his office; he had the intention of doing everything possible to help this young man. This young man in particular had a cynical self-egotistical attitude; no one could get through to him. After the young man was seated, the minister gave him an opportunity to speak, this is what he said, "I know you are going to tell me about my sins, how evil I am, my faults, my failures, repentance, faith in God and all that hogwash." He continued and said, "None of these things can help me. As a matter of fact, nothing you say or do or anyone else can help me.

The young man fully expected the minister to lash out at him for his bad attitude. He noticed that the minister he did not flinch once, while he was speaking. Then the wise minister spoke up and replied, "You came for help which is a good sign. I sat down and listened to you for over and hour knocking yourself and everyone else for your problems." Then the minister spoke said point blank to this young man, **"Son, the only person who can help you, is you."**

The young man took a long hard look at the minister; his eyes and mind opened up and instead of blaming everybody else for his problems, realized for the first time that *he* was his own problem. Tough as this young man was, he broke down and started crying as he poured his heart out to God. The minister let him cry as long as he wanted. When the time was appropriate, the minister counseled the young man and then prayed with him. The young man left the office a different person; most of all, he left with God's peace all because he opened up from the inside. After realizing he was the one standing his way and could not be helped before. He hugged the minister (something he would have done before) and he went on his way free and happy.

You cannot obtain help and be helped if you are if you are locked in. *You* have the power to control your own mind and spirit and *you* have the key in your hand; it is called your **will.** This might shock you but if you make up your mind to do something right and constructive for your future, and get out from the rot you are in, no one—no demon, evil spirit, voodoo spell, witchcraft hex, not even the devil himself—can stop you. The devil is responsible for all evil on this earth—he is to be blamed for a lot of things but believe me, with faith in God coupled with your **will** and **determination,** you can make it! You can pull yourself out!

Again, let me reiterate: the key to opening the locked doors are inside of you and it is your **will.** Have you heard the saying, "Where there is a will, there is a way"? All you have to do is constantly say to yourself, "By God's help, I will make it; I will get through this situation." Even as you are reading these few lines something on the inside of you is already being aroused. In spite of your circumstances, situation, problems, loneliness, rise up on the inside, and say by God's help I will overcome. I can make it, I am determined. Business deals might have fallen or fail, money ran out, you might be at the point of losing everything you own, people may or may not want to help you, however, you must remember you have to pull yourself out with God's help.

The Greek word for **will** is *Thelema*, which means "desire" or "whatever you want or want to be." In other words, it means what one wishes or is determined shall be done. It also means whatever we desire we can have according to God's will. Yes, people's ability, talent and knowledge are obvious, but they must be used for God's glory and to help you, your family and others. Remember, it's up to you can pull yourself out.

Lonely people sometimes have the tendency of accepting what is happening to them. If this is your situation, you must use your will power to combat the loneliness and circumstances you're in. When you do this your mind, soul and spirit will in turn respond positively to your life and to God. Your relationships will improve, and you will feel better about yourself and in societal circles. Then it's time to set some goals.

Recorded in the Bible is one of the greatest true stories of making wrong choices, ungodly living, shame, reproach, embarrassment and of course recovery and restoration. This true story was told by the Master Jesus Himself. He knew everyone and everything, He was God.

It is of utmost importance that these words of Jesus be written, so that, (one) the reader who does not have a Bible can read this story, (two) the reader would be inspired to have the faith like the young man in this story to be set free from the loneliness and other problems he was going through.

Here are the words of Jesus recorded in the Gospel of
Luke 15: 8-32,

And he said, A certain man had two sons:

And the younger of them said to his father, Father, give me the portion of goods that falleth to me. And he divided unto them his living.

And not many days after the younger son gathered all together, and took his journey into a far country, and there wasted his substance with riotous living.

And when he had spent all, there arose a mighty famine in that land; and he began to be in want.

And he went and joined himself to a citizen of that country; and he sent him into his fields to feed swine.

And he would fain have filled his belly with the husks that the swine did eat: and no man gave unto him.

. And when he came to himself, he said, How many hired servants of my father's have bread enough and to spare, and I perish with hunger!

I will arise and go to my father, and will say unto him, Father, I have sinned against heaven, and before thee,

. And am no more worthy to be called thy son: make me as one of thy hired servants.

And he arose, and came to his father. But when he was yet a great way off, his father saw him, and had compassion, and ran, and fell on his neck, and kissed him.

And the son said unto him, Father, I have sinned against heaven, and in thy sight, and am no more worthy to be called thy son.

But the father said to his servants, bring forth the best robe, and put it on him; and put a ring on his hand, and shoes on his feet: and bring hither the fatted calf, and kill it; and let us eat, and be merry:

For this my son was dead, and is alive again; he was lost, and is found. And they began to be merry.

Now his elder son was in the field: and as he came and drew nigh to the house, he heard music and dancing. And he called one of the servants and asked what these things meant.

And he said unto him, thy brother is come; and thy father hath killed the fatted calf, because he hath received him safe and sound.

And he was angry, and would not go in: therefore, came his father out, and intreated him.

And he is answering said to his father, Lo, these many years do I serve thee, neither transgressed I at any time thy commandment: and yet thou never gavest me no kid, that I might make merry with my friends:

But as soon as this thy son was come, which hath devoured thy living with harlots, thou hast killed for him the fatted calf.

And he said unto him, Son, thou art ever with me, and all that I have is thine.

It was meet that we should make merry and be glad: for this thy brother was dead, and is alive again; and was lost, and is found.

What is it that started this young man on his journey back home to this father's house? First of all, he realized the situation he was in, was not helping him or anyone but the pigs. Back home he had left a grieving family whom I believe were praying for him night and day.

What are the four words that he spoke that started his journey back home? It started with **"I"**. At this juncture of his life there were no family, friends or loved ones he could have spoken to, and his employer would have rather seen him eat the husks from the troughs that the pigs ate. Instead of offering him some decent food, he was more concerned about the pigs than a fellow human being.

Nonetheless, the prodigal reached deep inside of him and whipped up the courage to overcome his situation (which can be termed the "second wind") and he said within himself, **I.** an individual has to make up their mind if they want betterment and freedom from the adverse condition, they are in.

The other word was **"will"** the meaning of the word will, is the mental faculty by which one deliberately chooses or decides upon a course of action. One of the greatest boosters to a downtrodden spirit is your will. This is what started the ball rolling in the heart of the prodigal son; this is what prompted him to make his journey back home. It began when he had the will to go back home.

Then his will trigger his emotion to **arise.** The prodigal got up. This means getting up on "the inside" of you. Millions of people go to sleep on "the inside" of them. This is where major problems can set in. Naturally speaking, could you imagine a person that sleeps all the time, night *and* day? What do you think would happen to such a person? His or her blood circulation would slow down, followed by brain damage, then death. Many people are in a spiritual and emotional coma. The only way you can get out from your zombie like coma is to *arise* on the inside of you.

We come to the last of these four words: **Go**. Two letters, but what a powerful word! The four words spoken by the prodigal son were, **I will arise and go**. There is an old Chinese proverb that states, "He who would take a thousand steps must first take the first one." You been lying down for too long on the inside, if you will amount to anything is this life, you cannot allow loneliness or any problem to destroy you get up and **go**! Keep going until you find what you are looking for.

You do not have to succumb or give in because you have been lonely or bound up by any other problems. Life is filled with disappointment, but each problem, including loneliness, can be used as a stepping-stone or ladder to reach higher heights and deeper depths. Bowing down and being defeated then banished into nothingness and dying is not God's way. This spirit is coming from another source engineered by the devil to destroy you. Again, I tell you that suicide is not the way out. When this happens, the devil sits back and laughs, and says, "Yes, I have another soul."

The will to be down, discouraged, and considering death can be reversed by your will to live. No one can help you if you are lying down on the inside of you. It is true that you might be lonely but is no excuse, and reason for you to give up in life. It is true that sometimes the people you look up to will let you down, especially these days. Friends will turn their backs on you; loved ones might disown you; close family members will walk out on you; the plans that you made might not have materialized; business associates will run over you to get to the top; sometimes members of your immediate family will disrespect you and turn their backs on you.

But in spite of it all, with God's help and your will to live you will make it.

Doom looms over the individual and people that glooms, but on the other hand, no one knows like you do the adverse situation you are in—

the hurt, the disappointments, the frustrations, and the multiple times you have been let down but staying where you are is not going to help. Please remember that God Himself cannot help you; ministers cannot do anything for you; other professional people are useless to intervene unless you are willing to stand up on the inside of you and open up so you can be helped.

There's a story of a king in the Bible *Isaiah 38* named Hezekiah. God spoke to the prophet Isaiah to go and tell Hezekiah to set his house in order meaning to get things right with God for he was going to die.

What kind of attitude did Hezekiah develop after the prophet delivered God's message to him? He didn't throw up his hands and give up saying, "Well, I am going to die, I might as well go look at the best casket, pick out the best plot where I would be buried, call my family so I can see everyone of them for the last time as they witness, and I breathe my last breath. Then die, because there's nothing, I can do about it!"

It's recorded in *Isaiah 38;* King Hezekiah humbled himself and went to the church building, the house of God or the temple to **pray.** These temples were the kind of "church buildings that people could go in and pray any hour of the day. When he got to the house of God, possibly there were no priest, no music, no choir, no counselor, but he had a revelation that prayer changes things and he turned his face to the wall, prayed and wept. He asked God to remember how he served Him, how he was faithful to Him, he repented and of course he refused to die and because of him going to the house of God and praying and presenting his petition. God added fifteen more years to his life. The person you are looking at in the mirror is you, and no matter what the problems are in your life, including loneliness, are not reasons to remain in your predicament. Yes, the only person that can pull you out is…yourself.

CHAPTER ELEVEN:
HOW TO HANDLE LONELINESS

I have seen, read and heard so much about loneliness and how it is destroying millions of Americans and people around the world, but facts and figures do not help anyone. The reason for this book is not to show you facts and figures but to help you handle loneliness. The word, "handle" actually means, "Taking control over the situation." At this point, I would like you to understand that loneliness does not have to control you, but you can take control and conquer loneliness.

Recognize Your Condition.

The story about the prodigal son mentioned in a previous chapter, who demanded all of his inheritance from his father. After he received it, he spent it all in wild and riotous living. He ended up beaten, broken and busted, most of all he was lonely. The only company he had was the swine that he was employed to feed and possibly eaten pigs' food. Once he realized his state of being, he realized that he needed to change. What was it that changed his situation? The Bible said, "He came to himself"; in other words, he realized his condition and decided to do something about it. The same is applied if anyone is going to be helped.

Repent and Receive.

To some of you, the word repent seems harsh, but actually the word repents means to turn around and go in the right direction. After recognizing your condition and realizing you are in need of God's help, you must ask Jesus Christ to come into your heart. That's the first step in initiating the healing process in your life, including loneliness. "How do I ask God to come into my life?" Since Jesus already died on the Cross and the way to God was already made for you through His death on the Cross, His resurrection from the grave, you simply open your mouth and pray, "God, in Jesus' name, I come to you. I thank you for sending Jesus Christ to die on the cross for me. I repent for all my sins, and I confess all my sins "I receive Jesus Christ into my heart. I ask you God to wash me from all my sins, come into my heart, and dwell in me, Oh, God, by the work of the Holy Spirit. Give me peace, joy, happiness, and most of all; heal my body, spirit and soul. In Jesus Name: Amen.

The words that you pray do not have to be exactly like the above. But pray words that come from your own heart and mouth. As you pray, mean it. The moment you do this, according to the Bible, the Spirit of God comes into your heart, and you become a child of God. A supernatural act of God takes place in your heart and spirit, and from this point on you can experience peace, joy, and real happiness. Most of all, by repenting of your sins, you have started a relationship with God, please note (you have started a relationship with God).

*"But as many as received him, to them gave he power
to become the sons of God, even to them that believe on his
name." John 1:12*

Besides becoming a child of God, you have gained the best friend in the world, and you can start keeping company with Jesus. He certainly likes to keep company with you. After you have made this decision to walk with God, there will be days that you might not feel the same way as when you first got started on your Christian journey but remember; this is a walk of faith. HAVE FAITH IN GOD!

God Is Real; Prayer is Not Just Kid's Stuff.

Mention the word prayer to some people, and it's as though you have spoken a foreign language to some of them. Some people immediately think that prayer is only necessary when trouble is brewing. Some even think that prayer is just kid's stuff, but its certainly, it's not... We are dealing with the cure, accepting the cure for loneliness, how to remain cured of loneliness.

How many times have young people, in elementary, high schools, and Universities came back to their parents or pastors and say to them that they were called a sissy or a coward because they wanted to pray, read their Bible in school and they were laughed at or not allowed! It takes a real man or woman, whether young or old to pray and read his or her Bible in a public or private. No matter what anyone thinks, says, or does. These people have a desire for God, His presence and His power to help them.

What is prayer? Prayer is talking to God. It's that simple. It is like talking to the person next to you. God has given us one of the greatest opportunities and that is to walk with Him and talk with Him. Every believer not just the priest, pastor or evangelist has this blessed privilege but a believer in Christ Jesus.

As a Christian, you pray when you have difficulties, problems, and troubles, but when things are going good and you are healthy and in your right mind, this is the time to pray also. I apologize for the people in religious circles that have created the idea that prayer is just for folks in trouble. Prayer is having fellowship, communion and keeping company with God. He keeps company with you as well. You can sense the presence of God when you pray daily, and the beautiful thing about prayer is that you do not have to wait until you get to church (which is needed), but you can talk to Him anywhere and everywhere.

You will be surprised what prayer will do for you, especially if you are lonely. It was reported in a certain newspaper, that people who pray suffer less stress. One of our presidents was forced to leave office before his term expired, he was under great stress, because of the amount of excessive negative news that was circulating about his presidency; he was being hit from every side. He was under terrible strain and pressure from every side. The only people that stood with him of course were his family, friends and supporters.

During this difficult time, he called members of his staff and said to them "Let's pray." The news media got wind of this, and some reporters made fun of this, but they were not in his position. This man needed strength during this difficult time. Most of all, he was lonely. Loneliness sets in especially in times of difficulty and crisis.

There was no one else he could have turned to for spiritual strength except God. While most everyone was calling for blood this seems to be a trend when someone makes a mistake in this country, this president turned to God for sustenance. He was a real man. Real men and women are not afraid to call upon God at any time in any situation.

You are human; you were born with certain limitations. Even though mankind has the ability to accomplish great feats, do great things, such as sending a man to the moon, station in space where astronauts can stay in space weeks, months and more at each given time, send a letter and other important documents to any part of the world by the click of a button, communicate by audio and video to most any part of the world, and much more, yes! God gave man such understanding and knowledge and we must thank Him for whatever we have accomplished. We must never get to the point that we feel that we can function in any capacity without God. God has a way of letting us know that we need Him.

Praying to God in the name of Jesus can be of tremendous comfort to you. Taking time to pray is one of the most precious things you can do, for in prayer you gain strength, help, comfort, peace of mind, and a sense of safety. Prayer changes things, prayer changes circumstances, and prayer changes the atmosphere around you for better, prayer even changes you. I remember a song the adults used to sing when I was a little boy in Sunday school class; I grew up in church hearing them singing this song over and over. Then I felt the call of God in my life to enter the ministry, I have never forgotten this song.

By the way, most of the songs that are being song these days have no meaning; there are times its difficult to understand the words of some so-called Christian music. As a matter of fact, Christian music has become so commercialized and most of them lacks unction and the anointing of the Holy Spirit. Christian music with the anointing of the Holy Spirit has a way of drawing an individual closer to God. Here is the song that church folks used to sing, that remained with me to the present time, here are the words of this old church song,

What a friend we have in Jesus
All our sins and grief to bear.
What a privilege to carry
Everything to God in prayer.

O what peace we often forfeit
O what needless pains we bear
All because we do not carry
Everything, to God in prayer.

Have we trails and temptations
Is there trouble anywhere?

84

We should never be discouraged
Take it to the Lord in prayer.
Can we find a friend so faithful,
Who will all our sorrows share?

Jesus knows our every weakness
Take it to the Lord in prayer.

Are we weak and heavy laden?
Is there trouble anywhere?
Precious Savior, still our refuge
Take it to the Lord in prayer.

Do thy friends despise forsake thee?
Take it to the Lord in prayer.
In his arms He will take and shield thee
Thou will find a solace there.

Attending Church is not Just for Grandmothers.

Rid yourself of the idea that going to church is just for grandmothers and older folks. This is erroneous thinking. Going to church is for the entire family, single people, individuals, and especially, for lonely people. This is one of the best solutions for loneliness. Look for a church (a church is not a fine structured building), a congregation or body of people who believes in being saved or has experienced the born-again way of salvation through faith in Jesus Christ and are baptized with the Holy Spirit and baptizes in water by immersion.

Usually, this group of people tends to be friendly and have a genuine love for hurting people. There are other groups that are just as friendly but make sure that their teachings correspond with the teachings of Jesus Christ in the four Gospels and the teachings of the apostles. At the same time keep your eyes open for a pastor that believes the same, lives a clean life and cares for people.

In some larger congregations, it is possible to become obscure and unnoticeable or be lost in the crowd, especially if the congregation has thousands in attendance every meeting. This might not be the case in every large congregation but often is. True, you are not attending church seeking recognition, but it gives you a sense of belonging and people you can relate to and have fellowship with. This, in turn, strengthens you socially and spiritually. There are thousands of people that are lonely and hurting who are very shy about going to church. I learned this from counseling some of them.

Many lonely people have been disenchanted and are turned off by the negative attitude of certain people of different congregation.

Often though, there are some congregations who think that their church is only for the rich and famous, people of their class and type, their race, their color, and their background. Truly speaking, there is no such thing as a certain type of people church; the church is comprised of ALL people, above all else, you must choose a congregation that you feel comfortable with, and worship God and fellowship there.

When you attend church forget about the bad attitude of a few people; please remember they might be facing some problems just like you are. Break through that barrier and go with the intention and desire to worship and praise God, to hear the Word of God that will build your faith and help you have a closer walk with God. Become involved in the church outreach program, in reaching other people and meeting the needs of those around you. You will be surprised what a difference this will make in your life.

Throughout this book, it was stated that the first and foremost requirement in helping loneliness was to deal with it from a spiritual perspective. Now we will move on to some social aspects or some natural things you can do to help beat the loneliness syndrome. After God made Adam and Eve, the first man and woman he gives them the power of pro-creation that is to bring forth another human being into the world. Beginning from conception of the birth of a baby, humans go through the cycle of growing into man and a woman, God placed within every human being the desire of companionship with other human beings.

This of course refers to marriage and children, getting together with kin folks, friends and other people. Socializing is a way of life that is normal and healthy, especially in clean and wholesome relationship. It makes no difference who you are, and how spiritual you are; you need the company of other human beings. That's how God structured relationships among people. Never, never, never, get to the point that you feel you can do without your wife, husband, family members, loved ones, or any other human being, or some kind of human help or companionship. As a matter of fact, over the years, multitudes of people have become isolated from mainstream society. Ever so often you see and hear of religious groups taking off and hiding themselves in certain countries, mountains, deserts, and valleys. Some prominent people are becoming involved in cultish movements, but after a while most of them end up as self-destructive individuals or as a group.

Thank God for America. Regardless of what anyone might say its one of the greatest countries to live in, however, there are certain facets of our society that are developing a spirit of selfishness. The me and mine only attitude. The spirit of greed has taken over most people; there is a lack of communication among human beings. The spirit to compete, the desire to get ahead, this highly technological, computerized, beat the clock, mechanized, talking to computers and machines (which have no heart) society, has robbed human beings of appreciating one another. Humans are the only creatures that God made with a heart, (not the physical heart but a conscience, feeling, will, choice, love) cool it and begin to appreciate and love your fellow men and women and let's begin to appreciate and help one another. Reach out to someone especially if they are lonely.

Personally, I like the country and country people. Most people wave as they pass by, speak when they see each other, and answer the telephone politely.

Most of the time I am not afraid to leave my doors open, and if my car is broken down, someone will pull over and give a helping hand. This type of hospitality and helpfulness is missing from the people in most cities of America. I presume that people might be fearful, but God has a way of caring for people who cares about one another.

Comparing the people living in country areas to those in the city is like night and day. Most of our cities in America are beautiful places, but what really make a place beautiful is the people. But unlike the people of the country, most of the people in some cities will run over you to get where they are going. There seems to be no consideration for one another. Most of the people are rude; they will look right in your face and not even crack a smile or say a word, and it is considered miraculous if most of the clerks or attendants in business places smile or say, "thank you."

In so many big cities the honking of car horns is enough to send someone to the mental asylum and if your car is broken down on one of the highways and anyone stops to help you, it must be an angel! Because of this attitude in most of our cities, people are becoming withdrawn, elusive, fearful, and bitter. They are hiding themselves in their homes, apartments, and condos and wherever they live. Work is a must for millions of people; if they did not have to leave their homes to go to work, a majority of people will not venture out which is the cause of some loneliness. But you cannot allow negative attitudes to run you into seclusion for life. The only way to beat the negative is with the positive; come out from inside this shell, regardless of this attitude, and let your good be an example to others. Hiding will never solve problems. All of the above was mentioned without animosity and to propagate a change of attitude from the negative to a positive and help lonely people

Marriage.

Regardless of what anyone might say, marriage between a man and a woman and starting a family is one of the best ways of handling loneliness. Marriage is and will always be God's plan and directive for companionship even though the divorce rate is soaring. A leading organization conducted a survey and surprisingly a very high percentage of the people interviewed said marriage between a man and woman and raising a family is one of the most important things in people's lives.

This is how Almighty God planned, designed, and implemented His plan from the very beginning. When God made Adam, he saw that he was alone. He caused a deep sleep to fall on Adam, and then took a rib from his side and made a woman. God took a rib from the side of the man, this means for the woman to stand alongside the man, to help, encourage and inspire the man. Of course, the man has the responsibility of caring for his wife and family as they love and support each other, as they aspire towards their goal in life. Marriage is also for companionship, love and replenishing the earth. Notice that God did not take a bone out of Adam's head, so the woman could be the head or a domineering partner, but from his side to be of help to him, someone he can turn to in times need and loneliness.

Man and wife are to comfort and love each other in times of problems, pressure, and needs. God performed the first wedding ceremony and blessed Adam and Eve. Marriage was not meant to last one hour (heard of a couple divorcing half an hour after they got married) one week, one month, or one year but for as long as one of the partners departs this life. If you are single and lonely, marriage is second to relationship with God. It is God's plan and will for companionship. If you are single and lonely, pray, look, wait for the right person you will fall in love (not lust) get married and settle down in life, and raise a family. This is one of the keys of not being lonely.

My wife and I have been married (as of November 2014) for fifty years. Surely! We faced problems, (although not marital), but not one day has the word "divorce" entered our minds or was uttered from our mouth. If and when problems arose, we immediately joined hands and prayed to God for strength, help and guidance. Most of all, what a wonderful feeling it is to know that you have someone to share your life, your dreams, and your love with. You have someone you can trust and talk to when no one else is willing to listen to you. One of the greatest rewards of marriage is the feeling of knowing that your spouse will be there whether or not there is no one else to turn to.

Smile and the Whole World Smiles with You.

Do you remember the song "When you're Smiling the Whole World Smiles with you"? Believe me; it has been proven it takes more muscles to frown than to smile. Recently a leading weekly magazine devoted an entire page to this subject. The article went on to state that people who laugh are the happiest people. They are not tense, not under pressure, not susceptible to violence, and not likely to suffer with a heart attack. Even in religious circles today attendance will increase if the minister is serious about his relationship with God, firm in his beliefs according to the Bible, stands up for righteousness, meets their spiritual needs, *and* has a sense of humor and the ability to make people laugh! This is the reason the wisest man who ever lived, King Solomon, said, *"A merry heart doeth good like a medicine: but a broken spirit drieth the bones."* *Proverbs 17:22*

Whatever is going on inside of a person can be seen on the outside. People these days are so tense, uptight, and somewhat unresponsive. But smile anyhow; laugh anyhow. Choose company that are lighthearted, happy jovial, stay away from people that are sad, down, miserable, people who talk down and negative, also people who gripe, complain, critical and fault finding. But no matter what the situation keeps a positive attitude and a smile on your face. But just keep on smiling and soon it will catch on. There are times an individual might come into contact with people who are tense, serious and with a nasty attitude but just keep on smiling anyhow. There is a possibility that smile will catch on.

Go out and Meet People, Say Something Nice.

Why stay cooped up in a room day and night, unless an individual has to, most of the time this does not combat loneliness and increases depression. If you live alone and if it's possible, go out and meet people. Look for someone to talk to. Get out and walk. If everyone else might be too busy, go find a beggar or hobo on the street, (the right time and a safe place where they are) say and do something nice for him or her. You will be surprised how much this helps. I remember stopping at a restaurant with some company to get something to eat. There were lots of people in the restaurant.

Everyone was talking trying to get his or her point of view across to the other one. Waitresses were busily shuffling back and forth, the expression on the manager and chef's faces, were thankful for the business. We choose a table away from everyone and sat down to order. After a while one of the waitresses came over to our table to take our orders, and we noticed a sense of disgust on her face. She was not enjoying one bit of her work and what she was doing. I remember speaking up in the midst of my company and I said to her quite politely, "How you are?" She half-heartedly replied back to me in a very disgusted tone of voice.

Some other people would have walked out, because of the impolite manner in which she answered, but it dawned on me with the pressures of personal problems, caring for her family working on this tedious job of being a waitress. I spoke up, and asked her, "You all are very busy here at this time of the night, aren't you?" She responded, "Too busy."

Then I said to her, "If you think about it, your job is an opportunity for you to meet and know more people." She smiled and said she never considered it from that point of view. And then I told her it's a good night for her to up her tips ten times more Her eyes sparkled as she smiled again then in the midst of everyone at my table I told her I was a minister, I noticed she was under a lot of pressure but we will pray for her, by that time she took our orders, enjoyed our dinner, as we were about to leave that waitress gave us our check, she came back and told us she had just been through a divorce and was lonely, teary eyed she asked us to pray for her, and we did. She was a different person because I took the time to say something nice to her, some other people would have complained to the manager. But think for a moment this woman needed some comfort and encouragement. This is how God meant it to be, help and encourage to one another.

Get Involved.

During World War II, some of our American soldiers were taken prisoners and placed in concentration camps. As expected, some were tortured, some were beaten, some were starved and dehydrated, and some fell seriously ill because of the unsanitary conditions. Most of the soldiers became depressed, lonely and gravely ill to the point of death. It is said of the soldiers who took their minds off their own suffering and helped their fellow soldiers were the ones that survived the concentration camps.

Staying wrapped up in your own problems can hurt and can bring an individual to the point of chronic loneliness, as well as several other problems? Forget about yourself as often as you can and get out and help somebody who is in need of help. You will be surprised to see what a difference it will make in your life. Just by getting your mind off your own problems and troubles will make them seem inconspicuous. I have noticed when you help someone else someone else helps you and God blesses the individual who has a heart to help people in need. At a certain airport a flight were hours late, everyone waiting for that particular flight was so mad and disappointed, but this particular minister bought drinks and hot for everyone who was traveling on that flight, this deed cheered up everyone.

There is a story of a man who was complaining that he did not have a pair of new shoes and that the pair he had on were old and worn out, but just as he stepped outside, he noticed a man in a wheelchair who did not have any legs. He became embarrassed and from that point on he stopped complaining. You can join one of thousands of charitable organizations and start helping someone else, which in turn, would be a blessing to you also. Doing nothing leads to a life of boredom, unfruitfulness, and loneliness. God made us to be productive in every area of our life. Don't be afraid to do something; don't be afraid of failing. Failure is a way of saying "I can do better next time. I am going to try again until I am successful."

There are millions of people in America that are hurting; all they are looking for is someone who cares. All you have to do is take a trip to the nursing homes, hospitals, jails, rehabilitation centers, and alcoholic anonymous, etc. Walk down the streets of Miami, Detroit, New York, Atlanta, and other cities. Look at the winos, the homeless, junkies, prostitutes and drug addicts. Although they are trapped in what they are doing, most of them are crying out for help.

Share With Others Whatever God Has Blessed You With.

Everyone speaks of Jesus performing the miracle of multiplying the loaves and fishes to feed five thousand men; this did not include women and children. But very little is said of the little boy who was willing to give up his lunch of five barley loaves and two small fish in order to contribute to the solution. Droves of people followed Jesus and stayed with Him, even in the wilderness. At the end of three days the people were hungry; Jesus, of course, knew this. There were no stores in the wilderness, and according to Scripture, if He sent them away hungry, they would pass out on the way home. But because of one little boy who was willing to give up his dinner, Jesus took five loaves and two fish and multiplied the loaves and fishes and fed five thousand men. Historians believe that this multitude comprised of twenty thousand people including women and children. This miracle is a prime example and should serve as an encouragement to share what you have. Don't underestimate the far-reaching effects of your generosity and unselfish commitment to help someone else. Loneliness can sometimes breed selfishness, and a selfish person can be one of the loneliest of all people. If you are determined to triumph over loneliness you must come out from under your shell and start sharing what you have with those that are in need, give from whatever little you have, make someone else happy and you will be happy.

Walk in the Mall; Take a Stroll in the Park.

Staying behind closed doors can make your situation worse. You must get out and socialize to some extent. Select convenient hours; choose the places that are safe and go where other people are. Get out and at least say, "Hi," "Hello," "How are you?" You will be surprised how much this helps to overcome loneliness. Walk in the mall; approach a person that looks friendly and strike up some type of conversation. Speak to a friendly clerk, and other attendants. This kind of icebreaker will do wonders for you.

Fishing is one my favorite hobbies. If you go fishing, you will meet interesting people and hear wonderful stories such as the big one that got away, etc. Such stories bring laughter and do wonders for you what no medicine or psychiatrist would be able to do. Some of America's downtown streets and towns used to be the favorite pastime; people used to just take a stroll downtown. Recently, however, some downtown areas have become so unsafe, yet I noticed a lot of towns and cities are restoring the downtown streets, stores, and restaurants. Yours truly do a lot of traveling especially overseas, but one of the commendable things about going overseas (the countries that are safe for Americans to (travel) the people are happier. They make time for honest fun, and they laugh and enjoy life more.

Americans are under a lot of pressure; people here are tense than any other time in history. This is destroying our society but there are some towns and areas in America where I enjoy going. Of all cities that I have visited, Memphis Tennessee is the first city that comes to mind as one of the friendliest cities of America, (this of course was many years ago) Most of the people yours truly met in Memphis are down to earth and friendly, (I guess that's why Elvis lived there) and they will take time and talk to you. Conversing with friendly people helps you to overcome loneliness and depression.

Educate Yourself.

God made you and gave you a mind and brain. He gave you the tools necessary to improve yourself and to occupy your mind with healthy thoughts or ideas. Remember the slogan, "A Mind is a Terrible Thing to Waste"? Regardless of the prophets of doom concerning America, this country is still a great country to live in. Opportunities are limitless; there are so many libraries and books in abundance. Self-tutoring subjects are limitless, and certain training schools and learning centers are everywhere, even online. Put your brains, thoughts and mind to work. Harness them and become productive. The learning process never ceases. You should learn and improve yourself as long as you live.

What you put inside of you is what is going to come out; what you program yourself to be is what you are going to be. Stop thinking and talking about the adverse problems you faced in the past. Forget about them and improve your situation. I detest television shows that constantly project so much of the negative side of life. Once I glanced at a show and after a few minutes I had to turn it off. The show highlighted loose talk and loose living among men who appeared on the show, showcasing how many women these men went to bed with. It showed how certain lovers and families who were against one another, and they literally wanted to fight on the show. This show was not really an example for families.

None of this helps a person's mind. Instead, read books and view programs that are more beneficial and constructive for life and the future.

A certain mechanic that I met some time ago told me that he became a certified mechanic just by reading books on the subject as he worked on old cars. He added there was a time in his life where it seemed like he was heading nowhere. Lonely and dejected because his parents divorced at an early age, he suddenly decided he would go out and make something of his life. Because of his ambition and extra effort to help himself, he has a trade, a business of his own, and a fine Christian family and a happy life.

Pick Up the Phone and Call Somebody.

You are by yourself. You probably have already watched about three hours of television, which might mean a movie plus some other shows. You turn off the television set and lie on the bed or couch. So many things go through your mind; no one knows you are there, lonely and needing a friend. But talking to someone can help; please pick up the phone and call somebody and talk with him or her for a while.

This will help you feel so much better. God bless the millions of mothers all over America and other parts of the world. Mothers will listen when no one else will; grandmothers are a blessing and will listen when some mothers will not. There are even some ministries that have prayer lines or hotlines that you can call to talk to someone. Don't be lonely call someone. It will make a world of difference.

Be Hospitable - Invite Some People Over.

Everyone has the right to their own privacy, and this is understandingly so, but this type of "be by myself" selfish attitude does not last too long. Soon you would see the grim reaper of loneliness creeping in. Open up, be nice, and be hospitable once in a while. Dig up the best recipe you have and cook the best dinner that you can. Invite some people that you know, entertain and be nice to your guests. By evening's end you will have gained some friends.

Don't sit down in a corner and have a pity party because you are lonely. Certainly, some people have been nice to you in your life; do something nice for them in return and invite them for dinner. A person or family who just likes to be in the receiving end is never happy. Jesus said that it is more blessed to give than to receive. American citizens, just learn to love and appreciate and help each other all the time not only is times of crisis.

There are some wonderful people in this country everywhere especially in some smaller towns—but the statement that is about to be made is not to belittle America or Americans, but to help have a better relationship with one another and other people of the world. The following observation and statement is made from a constructive point of view and a heart of love: Except for a small percentage of the population, generally speaking, Americans are *not* the most hospitable people of the world. Now that I have your attention, please read on.

Honestly speaking, for those of you who will be traveling, have traveled, and are traveling, take an airplane and fly into any other country where it is safe for Americans to travel into and observe this: when in another country, most Americans develop a kind bossy attitude from the moment they step out of the airplane. However, for the people overseas, it's a different attitude altogether. Whenever Sherry and I travel overseas, the

CHAPTER ELEVEN: HOW TO HANDLE LONELINESS

people do everything possible to make us happy. Wherever they live, whatever little they have, they are always willing to share it with us. I am very appalled by what some people say when they travel overseas. They talk about the

They talk about the negative, and not the good or the positive. True, America is a great country to live in, but there are good in other people and other countries of the world.

On one of our missionary trips (the name of the country is withheld for certain reasons) Sherry, and I woke up about seven in the morning then departed and rode in a rented bus for about thirty miles. The paved road became a dirt road and finally, we came to a river where some natives were waiting for us with a few mules. We were scared of riding the mules except, but it was necessary in order to cross a certain river. Then we walked for eighteen hours nine hours going and nine hours returning. We walked up and down six mountains (these mountains we not real high mountains) crossed six small rivers until we reached our destination to top of the seventh mountain, our intention was to help some natives with some food, clothing, medical supplies, and most of all, to preach the Gospel of Jesus Christ to these precious people. This country's government hardly realized these people existed.

These people gathered in a shack made of coconut leaves for a church building. By this time the rain came pouring down, my wife and I spoke to the people in the rain (most of the people did not mind being in the rain). We spoke to them and led them to Jesus Christ, and then we gave them the supplies we carried to them. Words fail to express the joy and happiness we experienced upon seeing them so happy.

It was about 10:30 PM and after this meeting on this mountain, one of the native ministers and his wife invited us to their little hut made out of dirt and leaves. We insisted on going back due to the long walk down the mountains plus our bus ride to the hotel. Additionally, we had another meeting the next day scheduled in another city of that country. But the couple insisted we go to their little hut because they had already cooked some dinner for the entire missionary party and if we didn't go, I knew that we would have hurt their feelings.

Sherry and I went into the modest hut and sat down on some small benches; some of the guests sat on the dirt floor. As dinner was being served, we prayed for the Lord give us the grace to eat whatever was prepared. There wasn't any electricity, just a kerosene filled bottle with a wick call flambeau. With limited sight, I thought I recognized something that looked like chicken, plus some boiled green bananas. Whatever it was, we had to eat what was set before us. We started eating and the food went down slowly. Now we were thirsty and thought to ourselves, *what are we going to drink?* I noticed just a few feet from where I was sitting a hole in the ground with water in it. *Lord,* I thought to myself as I pointed the hole to my wife, *is that the water we are going to drink?* Then the kindhearted smiling lady host asked what we would like to drink (as her husband made sure we ate everything on our plate). As our interpreter explained her question,

I wondered I prayed to the Lord that the water in the hole would not be our drink.

Please remember there was no electricity, only a flambeau for light so we couldn't see very clearly. Then our host dipped her hand into the waterhole and pulled out a bottle with a familiar label: PEPSI COLA! We thought we were dreaming! The host pulled one Pepsi after another out of the hole as we each grabbed one and drank like crazy. So, you see, the hole in the ground with water was the only way they could have kept the drinks cool. By the way, these precious people had walked all the way up and down those mountains to get the Pepsi Cola for us to drink.

By this time, I was already choked up, as tears filled my eyes. I thought it was too much of a problem for them because they had gone out of the way to prepare for us. What really touched my heart about this entire mountaintop experience was that we had another nine hours of walking down those mountains, the man of the house spoke up again and said he was very concerned about us walking down the mountains this late at night. Then he said, "Please stay and sleep." I asked, "Where?" He replied, "In our house." I then asked my interpreter where the man and his family sleep would, to which he replied that they would sleep outside in the dew and the rain. At this point, I just felt like breaking down and weeping.

As we were departing our hosts told us that they were so honored to entertain and have us in their humble house. We thanked them again and left; I saw their tears and the disappointment on their faces and concern as we started to leave. I will never forget the words, kindness and hospitality of this man and his family.

Get out from the "Be by myself, wanting everyone else to do for you" syndrome. For once in your life, be nice and invite some people over. If you don't want to host a dinner at your place invite some people out to dinner at a nice restaurant or a beautiful place and enjoy their company which in turn would help your spirit.

Music.

Any normal human being should like some type of music. Music can have one of the most beautiful effects on your life. However, if you are lonely and listening to the wrong type of music, you will definitely become lonelier. Certain music causes deep depression and induces loneliness. Some music can create an atmosphere to do evil; some music can create an atmosphere for love; and then there is music that can inspire you to a closer walk with God.

Personally speaking, I like listening to a variety of music, especially the type that lifts my spirit. As a matter of fact, I have a collection of music from all the countries that I have traveled to. But my favorite music is contemporary gospel and some old black Gospel music which inspires me getting into an atmosphere to pray and worship God.

As a matter of fact, I like to go to a church where the music is upbeat and people loosens up dance a few steps or cut the rug some, then brings the worshipers into a point of worship and praise to God. All above lifts people's spirits and can help minister and do wonders for your spirit, soul, and mind, most of all can help lonely people.

Children.

Let me remind you that you were once a child, mother's little boy or daddy's little girl. How innocent you were! Then you became an adult and suddenly, the responsibility of your job or profession coupled with life's challenges placed immense pressure upon you. Unable to cope, you sought a place to escape from it all. Unfortunately, you spiraled into depression. A few days of depression turned into a few months then before you realized it, you were in a perpetual state of depression. Retreating from your family and everyone else is disastrous, and further plunges you into a web of loneliness.

Children can be a lifesaver especially to their parents, loved ones, and friends. Just as an aspirin can help a headache, most of the time, children can be a remedy when you are lonely. So many times, the responsibility of ministry has a tendency to place a lot of pressure on me, but I would get out of the house, office or church, and just play ball or something with the kids for a while. This really helped to alleviate the responsibility of ministry and some cares of this life.

Yes, some children are unruly; some are untidy; some step on your heart. Some causes you many sleepless night, but remember you were

101

once in those situations when you were growing up. But what joy they give you daily, watching them growing up, the loving things they did, some of the things they said, the questions they asked, the times they snook from into your closet and dresser and tried to look like you. My! How it gave you a bubbly feeling and laughter that only children can bring out of you

Quite a number of children have become victims of our society child abuse, incest, run-aways and neglected but this was not God's purpose, in giving you children. They can be best and greatest deterrent, comfort, and help in times of loneliness. There are times when you need to forget your responsibility, business, or job and take time and enjoy your children. Grandparents enjoy your grandchildren and take time with the children, talk to them, listen to them, laugh, run, and play along with them. What a difference it will make in your life and theirs. Don't be an old grouch, or a mean old lady, children are a gift from God enjoy them.

"Lo, children are an heritage of the LORD:
and the fruit of the womb is his reward.

As arrows are in the hand of a mighty man; so are children of the youth.
Happy is the man that hath his quiver full of them: they shall not be
ashamed, but they shall speak with the enemies in the gate." Psalm 127:3-
5

When the disciples started to turn the children away from
Jesus, He rebuked them:

"But Jesus said, Suffer little children and forbid them
not to come unto me: for of such is the kingdom of heaven."
Matthew 19:14

As a missionary-evangelist, while visiting a church during one of my meetings, I attended the Sunday school morning session. One of the teachers could not make it to teach her primary class so the pastor asked me if I would not mind filling in; he was surprised when I enthusiastically said, "Yes!" I enjoyed every moment of teaching that class and from then I wished I could do it more often. Teaching and being with those children for forty-five minutes gave me so much joy. I learned so much from them; their simple childlike faith taught me a lesson.

A five-year-old child was asked by her mother to pray before being tucked into bed. The mother watched her darling daughter as she knelt down beside her bed, and started to pray:

"O God, in Jesus' name I come to You. I thank You for guiding and protecting us throughout this day.

I thank You for my mother and father, for a house to live in, clothes to wear, shoes on my feet, and food to eat.

I ask You to bless my dad, mom, and my brother, sisters and please God make all bad people good, and all good people nice.

And please, God, take care of Yourself, or else all of us would be done for. In Jesus Name, Amen.

"What a prayer! Uttered from the mouth of a little girl.

Pets.

There is no substitute for God and human companionship, but for some people especially the handicapped, pets are the only tangible companions they have. In this country some have gone overboard with the attention that they give animals. It's a sin that adults can kill unborn fetuses and human lives are not valued anymore. Killing unborn babies is biblically wrong and taking a human life or lives could never be justifiable in the eyes of God. After an abortion and an apparent murderer, seems like the guilty individuals go free, but people go to jail for cruelty to animals. This does not justify animal cruelty; this is just an observation.

Dogs in particular can be helpful to some people and can become very attached to their owner. Animals, both dogs and cats can sense your pains most animals know when danger is nearby. Dogs especially are good to have around if you are handicapped and lonely.

Snap Out of it.

You have the power of choice. Whatever you choose decides your future and destiny. In simple language, if you choose evil, you reap the results of an evil life. If you choose God, you will obtain forgiveness, peace, joy, love, success, salvation, and healing. The promise of eternal life, living and dwelling in the presence of God eternally is conditional; all of this depends on the choice you make here on earth. You have to make a lot of decisions and choices throughout your life, and you can choose to remain in your loneliness, if you want to fight and learn how to beat it, you can.

It has been reported that seventy percent of the sickness that people suffer is self-inflicted, and is caused by doing the wrong things, eating the wrong things, drinking the wrong things, and going to the wrong places. Such is governed by a principle: your choice. Loneliness can be overcome, and if you are going to overcome it, there are choices you have to make. To begin with, secluding yourself from everybody else and having a self-help pity party is not doing you any good; you must stop this. Also, you must determine within yourself that no matter what! You will overcome loneliness because you can and with God's help, it's possible.

Before going any further, it is very important to interject these few Godly thoughts at this point of this book. Words have a way of making or breaking you. Words that individuals speak can make them or break them, destroy or build them up. The wisest man who ever lived who was King Solomon, who spoke these words taken from the KJV *Version of the Bible, Proverbs 6:2, Thou art snared with the words of thy mouth, thou art taken with the words of thy mouth.*

An individual must be cautious of words they speak. For example, I am not going to make it, I will die in my condition, this loneliness is going to kill me, it makes no difference what anyone says or does, my life is destined to be like I am. Words like these can bring a person to a gradual end.

To proceed, it was previously mentioned in chapter ten the story of the prodigal son. What is it that really triggered his decision when he spoke these words, *"I will arise and go"? He came to himself.* He came to himself, these words can be translated, snap of out it, sober up, get out of the wonderland spirit. When an individual is going through any type of problem or problems and its destroying one's life, there comes a time these demands a stern self examination. Say to yourself: is this situation helping or destroying me? If it's destroying you, then you have to come to your senses and sober up. Negative thinking and talking is never going to help.

I remember a noted minister and his wife married for over sixty years, she suddenly died. After the funeral he disclosed that he suffered severe depression and loneliness. He said he knew better than to let depression and loneliness bother him to an extent that it was destroying him daily. He mentioned "why I am allowing this loneliness to destroy me"? Even though he realized this is a normal thing to some extent, he said "he could not eat, sleep but just sit down and be complacent with deep digressional thoughts, like was I good to her, did I do her right". Even though he knew he did everything right in his marriage for sixty years. Thoughts like these were racing through his mind one hundred miles an hour. The devil can assumingly take advantage on an individual minds in times of bereavement, other problems and loneliness.

He said one day he woke up and said to himself, "I know my wife is in a better place, she is in the presence of God in Heaven, and then he said to himself this kind of thinking is not helping me or anyone else". He changed his thinking sobered up and went on to do what he was supposed to do for needy people around the world. With an attitude like this you are on your way to recovery, come to your senses and start your journey to total restoration and recovery. Just snap out of it.

CHAPTER TWELVE:
WHEN LAST DID YOU SING IN THE SHOWER, CAR OR ELSEWHERE?

When was the last time you sang in the shower, car, or anywhere? In a country where people are so tense, worried, and pressured in their homes while in traffic, at their workplaces, stores or businesses it was uplift to my spirit when I walked into a small business store and heard one of the workers singing. I smiled then commended him and said, "It's refreshing to hear someone singing in the workplace for a change." He attended to me, and we talked a little bit. Afterwards, he continued singing praises to God. It was a blessing to say the least.

People reflect the issues of their heart by the songs they sing. An associate evangelist and minister who traveled with me sang praises all the time. He said it made him feel great. What is singing? Is it just allotted for professional singers and concert artists to entertain people? No! America is blessed with some of the best musical artists; however, everyone should have a song in their heart that lifts their spirits because this combats loneliness.

Singing and music originated in heaven with God and His angels. Even now, the angels render praises to God and will continue to do so forever. Praise originated with God and will continue with God.

In America the music industry is a multi-million-dollar business, most of the time it is for a show and to make   money even among Christian artist. But since music, praise and worship originated with God and His Angels, singing to God and being thankful to Him always help an individual soul. People who praise God are people that are thankful and happy regardless of situations or circumstances. When you learn to praise God and sing praises to Him, you somehow release some pressure and doubts which in turn will help you and most of all honors God.

Since singing originated with God and His angels, singing to God and being thankful to Him is one of the greatest things any human can do, especially to overcome despair and loneliness. Singing and praising God is an honor that we should embrace and glorify Him with it. It is written in the Bible:

> *Praise the LORD; for the LORD is good: sing praises*
> *unto his name, for it is pleasant." Psalm 135:3*

> *Sing praises to the LORD, which dwelleth in Zion:*
> *declare among the people his doings." Psalm 9:11*

Someone might ask well how you praise God. After a hard day's work and you arrive at your home, affectionately greet your family. Freshen up enjoy a dinner before eating just say thank you God (its that easy) or a spiritual or Godly incline person would even go further and pray a prayer, and say God I thank you for allowing me to be home, I praise and worship you God for a good day at work, I am so thankful for a family and a home to come to, (sort of something like this or more), this in itself will do wonders for you and your family.

It must be understood when you have a spirit of praise and worship towards God, it reveals the type of person you are and what's going on inside of you. People who love's God and love to praise Him, these people are some of the happiest people in the world.   Why? They are giving praise to their Creator. One day, as I was driving from one place to another, I kept turning the radio dial, trying to pick up a Christian radio station, when, to my surprise, I heard the disk jockey say these words (and this was not Christian station): "To be alive is enough to thank and praise God for." There's so much we can sing, shout, and praise God for. We can praise Him for life, health, strength, food, clothing, family, jobs, some money to get by a place to live, a car to drive, etc. Once in a while it would do you good to get out from your apartment, house or office, and stroll by the ocean, look across its vast body of water. Or take a glance at the sun as it sets the full moon in its glory as it shines, the stars that light the skies and night. This and more are enough to cause anyone to sing, shout, praise and worship God.

Most of the psalms (songs) written in the Bible are laments and pleas for help from God. Many writers of the psalms also praise God for what He has done for them. Most of you reading this book have read and heard of the walls of Jericho coming down. This account is recorded in the Bible, the book of Joshua, chapter six (I ask you to please read it for yourself). How did the walls of Jericho fall down? The people who marched around the walls did not use battering rams and other means, and even if they did, it would not have helped because the walls were so wide, and part of the walls were buried deep in earth.

The walls of Jericho were so wide during those days they used to race chariots on top of it, but what is it that brought down the walls of Jericho? God told the children of Israel to march around the walls six days one time each day, and to march around it seven times on the seventh day. Then, while they blew the trumpets and shouted and praised God, the walls of Jericho come tumbling down.

In the book of Acts, chapter sixteen, some haters of true Christianity stoned and beat upon the Apostle Paul and Silas and threw them in jail. However, at midnight the jailed apostles prayed and sang praises to God. Due to their praying and singing God shook the jail and their chains fell off! Both men were set free to the amazement of the prison guard and authorities, this turn of events caused one of the guards to be saved and baptized.

From these references you will note how powerful praising God is, first of all praise frees your spirit and your mind. Furthermore, it causes your spiritual and natural walls to come down. If you are suffering from loneliness, praising God is the greatest thing you can do for yourself; it will help and set you free from your bondage of loneliness and bring you out of your spiritual and natural prisons.

Sports are one of America's greatest heritage and pastime. When one of our athletes wins a gold medal it makes us all happy. Thousands attend football, baseball, and basketball games during their season. What happens when one of the favorite teams scores a Touchdown, hits a home run, or sinks a three-point shot? People go crazy. They shout, scream, dance, and run. They run out onto the field and tear down goal posts. Why? It makes them feel good, that's why.

Such short-lived excitement makes one feel good some of the time, however, praising God makes you feel good all the time. When you develop a spirit of praise something is released inside of you. The joy of the Lord comes upon you. This is why I do not blame church folks when they get happy, as they sing, dance, shout, and praise God; it makes them feel not just good, but great. If you really want to feel great, happy and free, just go to one of the churches where they get happy; it will do you a world of good.

One of the worst things that have crept into the churches of America is the fact that too many of them have shut out the spirit of praise from the people. At some churches, the pastor does all the talking, the choir does all the singing, the musicians play all the music, the soloist does all the singing, and it seems like the preacher to all the talking or preaching. Communicating to the listeners is of utmost importance.

When people get involved and praise and worship God, this makes a world of difference.

Personally speaking, I like going to the type of church where you are free to praise and worship God, there are some of them where you see the worshipers shout, clap, lift their hands, sway with the music, some of you might not have heard of this type of language "cut the rug" and if you still do not understand it means "dance" yes dance in church, not the type of dance you will see in a disco pad or dance hall but like church folks say "dance in the spirit", this surely helps lifts your spirit, and lets off the pressure of. Just by lifting your hands and saying praise God, Hallelujah, thank you Jesus, you can feel the difference.

The best thing you can do for yourself is to worship and praise God ALOUD because it breaks yokes. Sing whenever you are in your home, in the shower, in the traffic, in church anywhere. Just try it, you will feel the difference.

Listening to others sing, praise, and worship might help a little. Hearing a recording of one of your favorite artists might inspire you. Personally speaking, I enjoy good singing and good music. This might even surprise you coming from a minister. I even like to see a good dance or dances done in a decent manner and clean atmosphere. But this will never help you until you learn to praise, sing, and worship for yourself. Here are some words from the Apostle Paul from the Bible, *Ephesians 5:18-20,*

> *"And be not drunk with wine, wherein is excess; but be*
> *filled with the Spirit, Speaking to yourselves in psalms and*
> *hymns and spiritual songs, singing and making melody in*
> *your heart to the Lord.*

> *Giving thanks always for all things*
> *unto God and the Father in the name of our Lord Jesus*

111

Christ." Ephesians 5: 18-20

On my way to Venezuela, I stopped at some of the West Indian islands and ministered in some of the largest churches. It was so refreshing to see the people coming to church to the meetings, singing and praising God. This was certainly a sight to behold. Some members did not have a car to drive, or any other type of transportation, but this did not stop them from coming to church singing shouting and praising God. I want to share with you the lyrics to one of the songs they were singing:

> *Hallelujah anyhow, Hallelujah anyhow*
> *Never never, let your troubles bring you down*
> *When life's trials comes your way*
> *Lift your head up high and sing*
> *Hallelujah anyhow*

A story is told of a poor little boy who attended a local church where people were really happy and knew how to praise and worship God. This little poor boy had a favorite seat where he usually sat down in that church. So poor was he that he did not have any shoes on and was barefoot in church.

One day, a fine dressed gentleman came to the same church and sat down beside the little boy. While the congregation was singing, shouting and praising God, the boy was clapping, singing and having a good time. The child was so noisy that the fine dressed gentleman could not stand it any longer. Finally, this gentleman said to the little boy (as he noticed he did not have any shoes on his feet), "If you will be quiet, I will buy you a pair of shoes." The child needed shoes so desperately that he quieted down. However, after a while, he could not sit still and do nothing. He looked at the gentleman and said to him "Sir, shoes or no shoes, I'm going to praise the Lord!"

This is the kind of attitude you need to have in order to combat loneliness. You must sing, shout, and praise your troubles away. This will help you overcome your problems and adverse situations that you are experiencing. This kind of attitude will propel you into a life of freedom and praise. By learning to praise God, you will conquer your inner fears and of course loneliness.

CHAPTER THIRTEEN
HELP IS HERE! THE HOLY SPIRIT

There are people especially professionals who want to be alone, possibly to work on certain project, and understandingly so. There are some people who choose to live alone because they want to. However, some people have no choice, and because they have no one, no home, and no family, they are out in the heat and cold. They live in homes, apartments, trailers, hotels, motels, truck stops, bus stops, rest areas, boats, the woods, parks, and even street corners and back alleys in certain cities. They are alone and lonely.

Once as I sat reading a national newspaper, I came across an article about how lonely people are and how they live their lives. Some of the people tried dating services (to no avail); one was a Vietnam veteran who was very lonely; another sat clutching her rag doll; one man was a millionaire yet battled loneliness and depression. By the way, do you know that there are approximately five million people older than age eighty-five up from 2.9 million in 1989? Some of these dear souls falsely presume that the only relief for them is death. Under no circumstances should one give permission to terminate a life regardless of how sickly or commit suicide. Only God has the power of life and death.

A minister whom I am acquainted with confessed that whenever he is finished counseling, ministering, weddings, funerals, meetings, services, etc. He comes home and finds no one at home or in the house, he said he finds somewhere to go until he realizes his wife, son, daughter or someone is home (he never goes home when there is no one there) Why I ask? These are his words "I am afraid of being alone or I get really lonely".

All of these illustrations and examples are not intended to magnify the problem, but rather, to lead you to the cure for loneliness. In a previous chapter, I shared how God used to come down in the cool of the day (that is morning and evening) to commune with Adam and Eve. God shared deep, intimate secrets with them; He instructed them on how to enjoy his blessings to the fullest. God made them that way, and most of all, if their innermost being and yearning was going to be satisfied, they needed His presence daily. This fulfilled their spiritual needs which gave them a sense of belonging and satisfied them totally.

Nonetheless, this privilege was marred by sin, yet God's love for His prized earthly creation mankind caused His Son, Jesus Christ, to die on the cross, and God opened the way for mankind to be reconciled back to God and to regain what he had lost in Eden. After Jesus died on the cross, He rose again from the dead and before going back to heaven to fulfill His Priestly duties, He promised to give us human beings further help.

As I stated, prior to Jesus' crucifixion, He talked to His disciples about the **Holy Ghost** or the **Holy Spirit**. Right here I would like to clear some fabricated misconceptions and misinterpretations concerning the Holy Spirit that has caused so much confusion in the minds of unbelievers, make-believers, and believers. It is the intent of the author to reach and help all people, and what I am about to mention is in no way intended to belittle, ridicule, or make fun of anyone's mode of worship.

Mention the word Holy Ghost or Holy Spirit and immediately some people think He (notice I said "He") is a wafer, water, oil, wind, or some kind of crazy manifestations or frenzy. The Holy Ghost or Holy Spirit is typically associated with people that are considered weird, odd, goofballs, holy rollers, snake handlers, etc. Some have branded the Pentecostals as "tongue-talking people"; some say that the Holy Ghost or Holy Spirit however you prefer to address Him is not relevant for today. Others have mentioned that in order for one to be saved, one must speak in unknown tongues, while another body of people says the initial evidence of being baptized with the Holy Ghost is speaking with other tongues, some say the Holy Ghost is love.

If you visit some of the charismatic worship services, you'll witness some of their members dancing, shouting, and singing as some of them kick their feet up in the air. Full Gospel Pentecostal ministers and people say they have the Holy Ghost by speaking in tongues, dancing, shouting, singing and running the aisle, however, many of them have nothing to do with ministers and people that are not believe like they do.

What was and is the purpose of Jesus sending the Holy Ghost or The Holy Spirit two thousand years ago. Recorded in the second chapter of the book of Acts? Jesus started preparing His disciples for the time after He leaves the earth and goes back to heaven. He knew the disciples would be persecuted, hated rejected, weak and lonely. These are His words as recorded in the Gospel of John:

> *"And I will pray the Father, and he shall give you another*
> ***Comforter***, *that he may abide with you for ever;*
>
> *Even the Spirit of truth; whom the world cannot receive,*
> *because it seeth him not, neither knoweth him: but ye*
> *know him; for he dwelleth with you and shall be in you."*
> *John 14:16-1 7*

One of the main reasons God sent the Holy Ghost or Holy Spirit is that God's presence which is the Holy Spirit will be **with you** and **in you** to **comfort you**. Webster's dictionary defines the word "Comfort" to mean, "Console" or "to gladden or make you happy." The word "comforter" comes from the original Greek word which *paraklesis*, which means "a calling alongside to help," or *paraclete* which means "one called along side to help."

What a wonderful God! Not only did He send His Son, Jesus Christ, to die on the cross; He also opened the way for you and I to commune and talk to God, to have a daily, living, thriving relationship with Him. He went even further to send us special help through the power and presence of the Holy Spirit, which in turn, would cause us to be consoled, comforted, and cared for.

There's no excuse for us to go through life problems in particular loneliness, trying to fight it by yourself. This is sufficient reason why people get into a quagmire of insurmountable confusion and problems one after another. Why do you think millions of people are so confused and face unnecessary problems all alone? With all of the medical breakthrough and professional help, there are more problems, sicknesses, diseases, and complications than ever before. Even though medical science has made some major breakthroughs there are more problems and sicknesses and people in the medical field cannot cope with insurmountable problems today. And can hardly delve into the minds and help people who suffer from chronic loneliness along with depression and oppression. This sickness is also a spiritual problem.

After Jesus went back to heaven, the disciples all one hundred and twenty of them—obeyed and went to the Upper Room in Jerusalem,

"And, behold, I send the promise of my Father upon you:
but tarry ye in the city of Jerusalem, until ye be endued
with power from on high." Luke 24:49

The disciples obeyed Jesus' command and gathered in the upper room, prayed, and worshiped God and waited for ten days until the day of Pentecost. Before this, the disciples were rejected, dejected, confused, troubled, lonely, and disillusioned, but on the tenth day, the Holy Spirit filled the upper room and the disciples, and they were baptized with the Holy Spirit, which changed their lives.

These disciples—some who previously had been afraid, confused, and fearful were suddenly infused with power to overcome the weaknesses of the flesh evil and Satan. They no longer harbored a spirit of fear within; they were no longer fearful of the Roman Government, or what their fate might be. Most importantly, they were not lonely anymore, because the Holy Spirit now was with them and lived inside of them. The physical Jesus was gone, but the spiritual, real, living presence of the Lord would abide in and with each of them forevermore through the Holy Spirit.

The Holy Spirit is given by Jesus to guide, lead, reveal, and open up your understanding about the ways of God. Most of all, He gives you power to live above sin, the flesh, and the devil. Again, I would like to emphasize that the Holy Spirit, is not a wafer, a cracker, or an emotion. Yes, at times He is symbolically portrayed as wind, water, fire, oil, or a dove, but He is God desiring to live in human vessels, to **comfort** and use us for God's purpose and glory.

> *"For the promise is unto you, and to your children, and to all that are afar off, even as many as the LORD our God shall call." Acts 2:39*

You can receive the Holy Spirit just as the early church disciples did. All that is needed is for you to accept what Jesus did for all mankind by dying on the cross on Calvary and rising from the dead. He died for every single problem that you face, to be with you and for you in times of uncertainty, hardship and distress.

Because, His Holy Spirit continually lives in the heart of every believer, His presence never wanes, never ceases. If you believe what I have shared about the death and resurrection of Christ and His love for you and want to become a believer, confess with your mouth: "Jesus, I thank You for dying on the cross. I accept into my heart as Lord and Savior. Come into my heart and save me. Wash away all my sins, forgive me for all the wrongs that I have done. In Jesus' name, I pray, amen."

After you have prayed this prayer, constantly praise and worship God and thank Him daily for saving you. This makes you a candidate to receive the Holy Spirit. Also share your testimony with someone else. Be a witness for what the Lord has done for you. This book is not specifically a teaching on the Holy Spirit; however, I would like to interject right here that I could not live this Christian life without God's salvation and the power and presence of the Holy Spirit.

There have been times of severe trials, testing, and persecution. There have been times when the pressure of ministry and personal responsibilities seemed overwhelming. There are also times when it seems like all the good that has been done is not appreciated. Believe it or not, ministers are some of the loneliest people in the world but thank God for sending the Holy Spirit. The greatest joy in life is to know that God Himself is with me through the Holy Spirit.

Life in the fast lane does not have to be tense and pressuring whether you are, poor, middle class, rich, a millionaire or a billionaire. Whoever you are, please remember that you are human.

Human beings were not created superhuman there are weaknesses, situations and problems that we face, but the greatest joy is help from God. God has already provided help through the working and moving of the Holy Spirit, all people have to do is turn to God for help and He will help. Just to eliminate some confusion from the minds of people, the Holy Spirit is not some mysterious being, but Holy Spirit is God, this is God's way of saying that you that we are human with human frailties, but when the Holy Spirit comes into an individual, He gives them strength most of all comfort in times of loneliness and other problems. The Holy Spirit is God's way of saying that you are not alone, I am with you through out everything that you are going through, and I am closer than you think, more so to dwell in you be in you. The Holy Spirit is to help you in all problems, including loneliness.

People obviously think that God is way up there and has nothing to do with human beings. There are certain religions that teaches that we human beings are too sinful for God to be with and especially live in us, but this is not so. This is the reason God sent Jesus Christ to die on the Cross, Jesus was the perfect sacrifice, and He paid the ultimate price for our sins. Jesus dying on the Cross was God's way of saying to us humans you should have been on Cross, but my Son died in your place and the Bible says He took our sins and nailed in on the Cross, then He rose from the grave went back to Heaven and He sent the Holy Spirit to be with us to live in us so that you will not be lonely anymore.

This is how the entire plan of salvation works especially if people want God to help them, especially people who are lonely. An individual comes to the author, and you say to me I am so thirsty, I desperately need a drink of water, I go and get the water in a pretty glass and then bring it to you, but you just stand there saying my! That glass looks so pretty, and that water looks so good, for ten minutes you stand in front of me saying the glass and the water looks so good, this obviously would do you no good.

Remember you are about to die of thirst, but not until you take the water from my hand and drink it, you definitely will not be satisfied. Talking about God sending His Son Jesus to die on the Cross, observing

His death and Resurrection is all commendable, talking about Jesus Resurrection and Him sitting at the right hand of the Father to make intercession for us, is certainly doctrinally correct. But please remember that Jesus did tell the Apostles, and this is for us today, that He would send the Holy Spirit and He will be with you and in you. The reason is, to help and comfort you, but you have to receive Him or God's Spirit, this is the only way you can be helped even in loneliness.

And I will pray the Father, and he shall give you another Comforter, that he may abide with you forever; John 14:16

Nevertheless, I tell you the truth; It is expedient for you that I go away: for if I go not away, the Comforter will not come unto you; but if I depart, I will send him unto you. John 16:7

Let us therefore come boldly unto the throne of grace, that we may obtain mercy, and find grace to help in time of need. Hebrews 4:16

CHAPTER FOURTEEN:
THE MAIN CURE FOR LONELINESS

From the book of Genesis Chapter Six, we learn that the human race had become so wicked that God decided to destroy mankind with a flood. However, before this happened, a man by the name of Noah found favor with God. Being the merciful God that He is, God spoke to Noah to build an ark to protect him and his family from the impending flood.

God desired intimate fellowship with His most cherished creation and was willing to give mankind another opportunity to live and enjoy life and most of all to live for Him. Noah obeyed God and did as he was instructed. After he built the ark, a flood came and destroyed the people of that day, except Noah and his family, which included his three sons, Shem, Ham, and Japheth and their wives. These families would give birth to all the families of the world. After the floodwaters receded, Noah and his family settled on the earth once again then the world became populated again.

Through the lineage of one of Noah sons, Shem, a man by the name of Abraham was born. God spoke to him to take his wife and separate himself from his idolatrous family by sojourning to a foreign land. Abraham obeyed and settled in the land of Canaan. Out of Abraham, God raised up the Jewish nation, who were the only people that knew the true and living God, and out of this people Jesus Christ, the Son of God, was born. An angel of God was sent from heaven by God's command to a humble virgin by the name of Mary. These were the Angel words to her:

"And in the sixth month the angel Gabriel was sent
from God unto a city of Galilee, named Nazareth,

To a virgin espoused to a man whose name was Joseph,
of the house of David; and the virgin's name was Mary.

And the angel came into her, and said, Hail, thou that art
Highly favoured, the Lord is with thee: blessed art thou among
women.

And when she saw him, she was troubled at his saying,
and cast in her mind what manner of salutation this
should be.

And the angel said unto her, Fear not, Mary: for
thou hast found favour with God. And, behold, thou shalt
conceive in thy womb, and bring forth a son, and shalt call
his name JESUS.

He shall be great, and shall be called the
Son of the Highest: and the Lord God shall give unto him the
throne of his father David." Luke 1:26-32

Please note that in the biblical record of the announcement of the birth of Jesus Christ, the angel specifically mentioned that Jesus Christ would help anyone who placed their faith in Him. God the Father saw that people were tired of tradition, rituals, and religions; burdened down. Most of all they needed a relationship with God. This became possible through the death and resurrection of Jesus Christ.

Jesus grew up in Nazareth among ordinary people, and, as the Bible says, *"And Jesus increased in wisdom and stature, and in favour with God and man," Luke 2:52.* At the age of thirty, He began his earthly ministry. His first miracle was turning water into wine at a wedding party, then He began to heal the sick, open blind eyes, unstop deaf ears, and most of all ate with and ministered to and forgave the worst of sinners such as harlots and tax collectors.

But what was the main purpose of Jesus Christ's birth? He didn't just perform miracles for miracles' sake. His life was more than miraculous deeds much more. His lifestyle differed from the priests and ministers of that day; He definitely met the needs of the people and solved their problems; He had a message, not a sermon; His message was not about a denomination, organization, or religion. Jesus had a message for the people of that day. What was (and still is) His message?

The message is this: God, through His Son Jesus Christ wants to be save mankind from their sins, sickness, and problems. Most of all God desires to dwell in mankind, so that the emptiness void and loneliness within the heart of mankind would be alleviated. He desires to comfort and care for us in every way possible. In other words, God desires to be with us and live in us; He wants us to trust Him in every in phase of our life. Is such a relationship possible? Yes, from a biblical and spiritual point of view. In the *3rd* and *4th* chapters of the *Gospel of John,* Jesus ministered to two people and Nicodemus and the woman of Samaria gave them two greatest revelations necessary to solve their innermost longing desire for satisfaction and to help solve their problems. These revelations are certainly for us today.

Jesus Christ redeemed mankind from all sins and open the way for mankind to have God's spirit and presence in our lives. This was planned and determined by the determinate council of God from the very beginning of time. Adam and Eve sinned against God. This obviously means that the birth of Jesus Christ was not coincidental. In the book of *Genesis 3:15* we read, *"And I will put enmity between thee,* (people, born through and after Adam and Eve, with the sinful nature, caused by the fall, through Satan) *and the woman,* (referring to Jesus Christ who would be born of Mary, through the power of the Holy Spirit)." through the power of the Holy Spirit)."

The above prophetic Scripture was fulfilled when Jesus was born, and He lived among His family and experienced a home life among siblings and parents. He also attended the local synagogue to worship God, hear the word of God, and fellowship with God's people. On one particular Sabbath day, the priest handed Jesus the "Torah" the Jewish "Bible" or scroll with *Isaiah's* prophesy and Jesus stood up and read:

And he came to Nazareth, where he had been brought up: and, as his custom was, he went into the synagogue on the sabbath day and stood up for to read. And there was delivered unto him the book of the prophet Esaias. And when he had opened the book, he found the place where it was written,

The Spirit of the Lord is upon me, because he hathanointed me to preach the gospel to the poor; he hath sent me to heal the brokenhearted, to preach deliverance to the captives,and recovering of sight to the blind, to set at libertythem that are bruised, To preach the acceptable year of the Lord.

And he closed the book, and he gave it again to the minister, and sat down. And the eyes of all them that were in the synagogue were fastened on him. And he began to say unto them, This day is this scripture fulfilled in your ears.
"Luke 4:16-21

As recorded in all four Gospels, Jesus preached the Gospel to the poor in spirit; this means all people that were humble enough to receive the Gospel. He healed the brokenhearted and opened the eyes of the spiritually blind. Their eyes were opened to God's provision of salvation for them. Jesus preached that He came to help and deliver mankind from their problems and needs but He came to teach that God wants to dwell in mankind, but He went further than any man did, Jesus showed His love for mankind by dying on the cross and rising from the dead.

There were many religious and pious people in ages past such as Confucius, Buddha, and Muhammad—even popes, kings, queens, Krishna, and others who came to live but Jesus was the only God man who came to die.

Jesus freed men and women from the bondage and curse of sin. His words, spoken in the above Scripture were fulfilled exactly as He announced. God has not changed His mind concerning deliverance for people. He wants to do the same today as He did for people in past ages. What really happened when Jesus died on the cross? Jesus did not only come to live but also came to die and resurrect from the grave. After three years of ministry in Jerusalem and surrounding areas, prior to His crucifixion, Jesus gathered with the Apostles in a large upper room.

A solemn gathering it was. During this last supper Judas Iscariot, one of Jesus disciples betrayed Him with a kiss on the cheek. After supper Jesus and His disciples went to the Garden of Gethsemane where He prayed so hard that sweat came out from His body as drops of blood *Luke 22:44. "Father,"* He prayed, *"if it be possible, let this cup pass from me."* He sensed the impending excruciating pain and realized the awesome death that awaited Him; He was going to die as a common criminal on a rugged Roman Cross.

The Roman soldiers arrested Jesus and took Him to Pontius Pilate's Judgment Hall. There they tied His hands behind His back and, taking a whip with tongs of lead on the end of it, whipped His back and dragged the whip across His flesh. As the blood flowed and bones were exposed, the soldiers pressed a crown of thorns into His head as far as it could go as blood oozed out.

Then they accused Him wrongfully (based on false accusation accounts and lies of the "religious" leaders) and condemned Him to death as a common criminal, after which began His long and tedious journey to Calvary to be crucified.

With the load of the heavy cross on His opened flesh and bleeding Back! Step by step, the Son of God willingly went up Calvary's Hill. A certain man by the name of Simon of Cyrene was forced to help Jesus carry His cross. The Son of God stumbled up to Calvary's Hill to bear the sins of the world. Crowds of people lined the road as they looked on in shock, many mocked while his followers and cried and wailed.

At Calvary's Hill, Golgotha, which is interpreted "The Place of the Skull," the cross was laid on the ground and the Roman soldiers positioned the bleeding body of Jesus on the cross. Then they took His right hand and a large nail and maliciously nailed his hand to the cross; they did the same to His left hand. His feet were doubled one on top of the other and a larger spike was nailed through both feet and fastened to the cross.

After lifting up the cross, the soldiers jerked it down into an existing hole. There, stretched on the cross and hung the Son of God, humiliated in front of family, friends, and followers, as his bloodthirsty enemies shouted, jeered, mocked, scoffed and laughed. Many Jews shouted, "Crucify Him, crucify Him," and taunted Him by declaring, *"If thou be the Son of God, come down from the cross" Matt. 27:40.* The apostles and disciples looked up in bewilderment, and wept for Jesus, as they realized, this is why He came: to die for them and the sins of the world.

As recorded in the Gospels, while Jesus hung on the cross a Roman soldier thrust a spear into Jesus' side and blood and water gushed out. This signified His grief for a lost and dying world.

While Jesus hung on the Cross in pain and agony, the devil thought he had engineered a perfect plan to annihilate the Son of God, but he did not realize the significance of Jesus' crucifixion. This was the beginning of God's perfect plan for **redeeming and reconciling mankind back to Him.**

And about the ninth hour Jesus cried with a loud voice, saying, Eli, Eli, lama sabachthani? That is to say, My God, my God, why hast thou forsaken me?

Some of them that stood there, when they heard that, said, This man calleth for Elias. And straightway one of them ran, and took a sponge, and filled it with vinegar, and put it on a reed, and gave him to drink.

The rest said, let us see whether Elias will come to save him. Jesus, when he had cried again with a loud voice, yielded up the ghost.

And, behold, the veil of the temple was rent in twain from the top to the bottom; and the earth did quake, and the rocks rent." Matthew 27:46-51

"It was now about the sixth hour, and darkness came over the whole land until the ninth hour, for the sun stopped shining.
And the curtain of the temple was torn in two."
Luke 23:44, 45
"When he had received the drink, Jesus said, "It is finished."
With that, he bowed his head and gave up his spirit."
John 19:30

You might be thinking, "What does the death of Jesus on the cross, and all of these Scripture references have to do with loneliness?"

Certainly, here lies the key to solving all of mankind's problems and of course loneliness. Jesus death on the Cross was not just to observe rituals, traditions, traditional prayers, wearing symbols of the Cross, counting of beads, observing Good Friday's, all of this is commendable, (and these statements are in no way condemning criticisms of people's religion) Believe me, all Fridays and other days will be good (spiritually speaking) when an individual understands the purpose of Jesus death on the Cross.

When Jesus died on the cross, He died for the sins of all people. He provided salvation this means to be free from the penalty and guilt of sin. This also means that on account of Jesus' death on the cross, a way was provided for you to obtain, peace, joy, contentment, and real happiness. Jesus' sacrificial death was God's way of saying, "Now you can live the way I intended for you to live from the beginning."

All of your problems, needs, sicknesses, diseases, broken heartedness, oppression, depression and loneliness and everything that humans go through, was and is already paid for by Christ's death on the Cross. His resurrection and ascension solidified and confirmed He was God. The moment you repent of your sins, and accept Jesus Christ as your Lord as Savior, these spiritual benefits are activated in your life.

Please recall that prior to the death and resurrection of Jesus Christ, in order for men and women to access God; they had to go to the priest so that an animal offering of some sort (sheep, goat, and dove, etc) had to be sacrificed on their behalf for the forgiveness of sins. Every year the people had to be purified of their sins if they aspired to have peace with God. But since Jesus died on the cross, no one has to do this anymore. He was and is the perfect sacrifice.

Jesus death on the Cross was the only sacrifice for the sins of mankind. No other sacrifice is accepted after Jesus died on the Cross.

The key to defeating loneliness and of course, all other problems is to be in relationship with God through His Son, Jesus Christ. Only then can a person be empowered to overcome the negative and demonic influences of depression and loneliness. This battle cannot be won without God's help. Please remember when Adam and Eve sinned, they had certain privileges and a daily, living relationship with God. But after they sinned, they lost their intimate relationship with God and so did every human being that was born after them.

From the records of Old Testament, God moved upon, or inspired, prophets, or sent angels to communicate with man. Some had direct visitations from God. Others had to sacrifice animals, burn candles, go through certain rituals, formalities and traditions to appease their sins, to hear from, and to have peace with God. Generally speaking, mankind was alienated from God. Also, the entire human race was cursed as mentioned in the previous chapter.

The entire human race was separated from God. I would like to expound two important Scriptures. In *Matthew 27:51*, we read, *"And, behold, the veil of the temple was rent in twain from the top to the bottom"* and *John 19:30 "It is finished."*

What do these Scriptures mean and what does it have to do with loneliness? Go back with me briefly to some necessary Biblical history. When Moses led the children of Israel from Egypt into the wilderness on their way to Canaan, or the Promised Land. Moses became their prophet and chief spokes person for God. The children of Israel had no way of meeting with and hearing from God, other than hearing what the prophet Moses told them. But God wanted to meet and commune with His people.

He instructed Moses to erect a tabernacle in the wilderness. This tabernacle was made of the finest purple and linen that was held in place with brass poles. There was one door for the priests to enter in. Upon entering, there were the brazen altar of sacrifice, large basin-like container filled with water for cleansing and purification. Then there were the outer veil, tables of showbread, the holy place, alters of incense, then Inners Veil, this veil is where the high priest alone could enter "The Holy of Holies". The Holy of Holies is where the Ark of the Covenant was laid and where the presence of God dwelt.

Between the Holy Place and the Holy of Holies was a THICK VEIL, which separated the holy place and the Holy of Holies. No one except the high priest alone could enter the Holy of Holies; this meant that all other people could not come into the presence of God. Only the high priest was allowed to enter THE HOLY OF HOLIES.

For about two thousand years, God, His power and presence was hid from all of mankind except to speak to certain prophets, priest and certain leaders recorded in the Bible. When Jesus died and gave up the Spirit a supernatural act of God caused this veil to be "rent in twain" or to be separated in the middle. This also meant that ever since Jesus died on the Cross to the present time, **every human being has the privilege to approach God and pray to Him for themselves.** When Jesus died on the Cross, His Spirit (God) came out of the flesh Jesus Christ of Nazareth, then His Spirit rose again and went back to Heaven, and now He is sitting at the right hand of the Father making intercession for you and me and of course all people of the world has **direct access to God, and could come to God for themselves and pray and worship God.** For the first time since Adam and Eve sinned in the Garden of Eden **all of mankind has a direct access to God.**

The death and resurrection of Jesus Christ means that all people regardless of race, color, ethic background, culture, or country can approach God directly for themselves. Jesus opened the way for you to come to God for yourself, talk to God, and have a living daily personal relationship with God.

Just before Jesus died, He uttered these words: *John 1930 "it is finished."* The purpose of His birth, death, and resurrection embodied the task of reconciling mankind back to God. Thus, His words symbolized that His task was accomplished. Now you can have God's presence and power with and in you; you can walk and talk with God, anywhere, and everywhere. Having a daily, personal relationship with God is taught to believers by the words of the Apostle Paul: from the Bible.

> *"That at that time ye were without Christ, being aliens from the commonwealth of Israel, and strangers from the covenants of promise, having no hope, and without God in the world:*
>
> *But now in Christ Jesus ye who sometimes were far off are made nigh by the blood of Christ.*
>
> *For he is our peace, who hath made both one, and hath broken down the middle wall of partition between us;*
> *Having abolished in his flesh the enmity, even the law of commandments contained in ordinances; for to make in himself of twain one new man, so making peace;*
>
> *And that he might reconcile both unto God in one body by the cross, having slain the enmity thereby: And came and preached peace to you which were afar off, and to them that were nigh.*
>
> *For through him we both have access by one Spirit unto the Father. Now therefore ye are no more strangers and foreigners, but fellow citizens with the saints, and of the household of God." Ephesians 2:12-19*

The truth of the death of Jesus and His resurrection is hardly being taught. This Gospel truth can revolutionize your life and the church world, and of course, reach the world. I saw a bumper sticker on a car that read, "God is alive and well, I spoke to Him this morning." This is powerful; this means the way is wide open for you to obtain and maintain a relationship with God. You will never be lonely again.

When God is missing in your heart and life everything you desire and want, even life itself, would be meaningless and void. You might try everything, own everything, and even have millions of dollars. You might even try your way and the way of others, but you will never find what you are looking for. Worst of all, there will be emptiness on the inside of you. You will never find what you are looking for until you accept God's way, and that way was made when Jesus died on the cross and rose again from the dead.

One the most powerful Scriptures in the Bible is found in the Bible

Hebrews 4:14-16, It reads:

"Seeing then that we have a great high priest, that is passed into the heavens, Jesus the Son of God, let us hold fast our profession.

For we have not an high priest which cannot be touched with the feelings of our infirmities; but was in all points tempted like as we are, yet without sin.

Let us come therefore come boldly unto the grace that we may find mercy to help in the time of need.

There are no excuses to suffer from any kind of problems, sickness, troubles, heartache, and most of all, **loneliness.** The way to God is to accept the answer—Jesus Christ. God is the best company you can keep; and the way to God is through Jesus Christ. Jesus sacrificial death on the Cross was consummated to accommodate every problem that human beings go through. This is how God wanted to reveal to the world how much he loves human beings who He created; God showed who He is through Jesus Christ.

Jesus knows what humans go through. He knows that we are flesh, with human frailties, weaknesses, as long as we are in the flesh there are going to be problems, but His death on Calvary was a perfect sacrifice for us to become perfected while we are here on earth.

Regardless of what you are going through as a human being, you do have some one that is higher than you are, who were human like you are, how you think Jesus felt?, He knows what it is to be hungry, thirsty, weary and lonely. When He was arrested in the Garden of Gethsemane, all of His disciples forsook Him and fled, one of them denied Him, yes, He felt lonely, and this is where you come in, if you are lonely. He Jesus has the cure for you. Choose God through Jesus Christ for He is your cure for every problem and of course loneliness.

CHAPTER FIFTEEN
EVERYONE CAN PRAY

Every one can pray if they would like to. In chapter four of this book, page ninety, mentioned was made of the importance of prayer and praying. Prayer is one of the best antidotes for people who suffer from loneliness. Reading books about prayer, hearing sermons about prayer, teaching on the subject of prayer, telling someone you are going to pray for them is commendable, but nothing could substitute when an individual can learn and know how to pray to God for themselves.

To begin with, the reader would recall in the previous chapter that it was stated that when Jesus died on the Cross, He died for every single problem that human beings face daily. Jesus died on the Cross for us to have peace, joy, happiness, contentment; an individual can also obtain forgiveness of sins, guilt and shame and have eternal life. But most of all when Jesus died on the Cross, He open the way for each and everyone to pray to God for themselves. Ministers are important but the responsibility of every minister is to teach people how to have a personal relationship with God. And this can be done by praying.

The author is taking you through, a point-by-point step by step principles where you can develop a relationship with God and pray to Him any time you desire. This is not a book on prayer, there are thousands of books on prayer but as was said earlier reading and hearing sermons on prayer are important, but prayer is such a Godly aspiration that an individual who is going to be spiritually satisfied, content, must have a knowledge of prayer and most of all pray to God for themselves.

Prayer is being alone with and God. You are talking and having fellowship with God. Is this possible, yes!

Jesus gave Himself as a perfect sacrifice when He died on the Cross. He opens the way for every human being to approach God. Anyone who desires to pray can pray to God for themselves. And they can do so any time, any minute, any hour, any day and anywhere.

Now, saying prayers and praying to God is like night and day or two different things. There times certain people because of their religious beliefs travel thousands of miles and spend thousands of dollars to pray in a certain place little realizing that they can pray to God right where they are and in the privacy of their home, no condemnation to any one's religion, but the people who does this shows clearly that people are desirous of God and wants to worship Him. People that are searching for God would try anything or everything to satisfy the desire to pray and worship God.

Much can be written about each heading that follows but these would be stated briefly so the reader can get an idea how to pray, -

HOW TO PRAY?

Before giving the reader an idea how to pray? It must be understood that there are two kinds of praying,
(1) Praying to God by your self or personal devotion
(2) Corporate prayer, this of course is praying together with other people in a gathering, meeting place or church building, etc.

DESIRE TO PRAY,

the only possibly way the author can explain "a desire to pray" is giving an example of himself. The author grew up having knowledge of the Bible especially the teachings of Jesus Christ and the Apostles. At the age of fifteen accepted Jesus as his Lord and Savior, at that moment the author felt a deep-down transformation occurred within his being. From that moment to the present time the author has always had a **deep-down desire and yearning within his being to pray to God.** But there are times the author just wanted to be alone with God.

Generally speaking, there should be a longing, desire, wanting, yearning to be alone with God, and to be in His presence and to worship and pray.

Sunrise and especially Sunset this trigger within the author's spirit and soul, a greater desire to pray. This much said if an individual has God in him, he will want to be with God. Desiring to pray is very important, this shows there is something inside of your spirit crying out for your Maker as you must take and spend time with God.

TAKE TIME TO PRAY!

God has given us life; the breath we breathe comes from him, the moment that breath leaves a person's body they go of into eternity. Humans should always be thankful to God for everything, and this is the reason there should be no excuse. When a person wakes up in the morning, the first thing that they should do, is to thank to God for **life.** To be alive is enough to thank God, take some time to pray or spend some time with God.

FIND A COMFORTABLE PLACE TO PRAY,

to be alone with God is one of the greatest opportunities we have, but what did Jesus say about a place to pray, *Matthew 6:6, But thou, when thou prayest, enter into thy closet, and when thou hast shut thy door, pray to thy Father which is in secret; and thy Father which seeth thee in secret shall reward thee openly.* Choose a particular place where you can pray each day. This place can be your bedroom, living room or some other particular room in your house. I have heard of some individuals turning their garage into a prayer room. You can pray in the yard, the open air, by the pond, lake, woods, or while driving or park in a convenient or safe place to pray. You want a place where you can get away from everything, everyone. The author is fortunate and thankful to God that I have a room in our home particularly separated to pray and to be alone with God.

READ THE BIBLE,

before praying one of the best thing a person can do, while preparing to pray is read the word the Bible. The best way to do this, is to read the Psalms, the Gospels, the words of Jesus, this is very inspiring. But whatever scriptures encourages and builds faith and inspires a person to pray this is advisable and feasible before praying.

PRAISE AND WORSHIP,

some one might ask what next after reading the word of God the Bible. Develop and spirit of praise and worship, praise and worship goes this way, God I worship you, God I praise you, God I thank you, I give you praise, honor and glory, Hallelujah, I love you God, thank you so much for life, health, strength, your love, mercy and grace, etc. You can do this as long as you desire, by then you will have already experienced the presence of God, how do you know the presence of God? The presence of God is a feeling of peaceful warmth flowing all over you, there are times the presence of God is like light volts of electricity going through your body, (if you do not sense or feel this that does not mean that God is not there) just keep praising or worshiping God anyhow. Worship God until you are filled with His presence and are satisfied.

BEGIN TO TALK TO GOD, TELL HIM EVERYTHING THAT IS IN YOUR HEART,

praying simply is talking to God, in a talk to Him like you would talk to your husband, wife, family members or a friend. If you find yourself crying, weeping and praying this of course is normal. At this point in prayer, talk to God about all of your problems, hurts, needs, situation in your home, pray for your wife, husband, children and kin folks, officials, the President. Pray for people who are poor and in need (with the intention to help them), pray about situations around the world.

Please remember this is just giving you an idea of how to pray, while in prayer the Holy Spirit can lead and guide you even into a deeper and wider scope of praying or prayer. Since this book is about handling loneliness pray and asks God to help you in your loneliness! God and prayer do help people who are lonely. Don't complain or pray negative prayers but be positive in your praying.

Pray to God like you really want Him to answer your prayers. Prayer can be such a release from the pressures of life. If people would pray more, they will live happier lives. Some Scientists are now discovering that people who pray lives stress free lives.

It must be mentioned at this point that there are people whose lives are so hectic they are on the go from morning noon and night. But you cannot be to busy for God. Stop and take some time to pray you can pray while driving, flying or sailing. Taking some time with God this can be more meaningful to your life; a friend of mine said these words "you cannot afford not to pray".

*The author is doing everything possible to help people in every way especially those who are lonely. Lonely people have the tendency to worry, worry, worry. While lecturing, preaching, teaching, it is a policy of mine to break down the tense feeling in people and the atmosphere. But I do get a chuckle, some laughter and smiles talking about people who worry. I would tell my audience you have heard the statement "why worry when you can pray" but I simply turn this statement around and quote it this way "why pray when you could worry" translated, people do more worrying than praying. A person who desires to pray, do not have to get into a traditional ritualistic rut or pattern of praying all the time. But pray and pour your heart out to God as you would talk to a lawyer, doctor, psychologist or talk to God as a friend.

SPEND TIME WITH GOD;

Prayer really is a privilege, a privilege to be in the presence of God, it is true that prayer is talking God about all of our problems, needs and situations; it is not complaining, explaining and traditional phrases and fanciful sentences to impress God or anyone else. But just to be in the presence of God is worth more than anything in this world. Privilege and awesome are the words to **be in the presence of God**. Problems, needs, circumstances and situations are the reason to pray, but just being with God is worth it all.

How do you think Jesus felt? Jesus built one of the largest congregation and followers. Jesus did everything possible to minister and to help people. When they needed to understand God more, He opened up their upstanding, those who needed to figure out how to be born again He penetrated their spirit opened up their hearts so they could understand or see what He was speaking about. He multiplied bread and fish twice to feed the multitude in the wilderness, why did He do this? Because He wanted to show He can do miracles, no, He cared and had compassion on the people, because they were in the wilderness hungry and He gave those people fish and bread to eat. To the working men who could catch no fish He told them where to cast their nets and they caught more fish than they did before. People who were outcast and lonely He disregarded the attitude of the self righteous and super so call spiritual leaders, to spend time with and comfort them.

To those who had no friends He became friends with the publicans and sinners, the woman that was caught in adultery when every one had forsaken her and was about to stone her to death, He did not condemn or left her to die, but words of comfort like "neither do I condemn thee go and sin no more" guess what she became His greatest follower and the first person (a woman) to break the news that He Jesus was alive.

All those who were sick He healed them, to the out cast and condemned He picked them up, when everyone ran away from a leprous person (people suffering from a skin disease called leprosy they were lonely and had to stay by themselves) but Jesus had the love and compassion for them then stretched out His hands and touched them (by law no one were supposed to touch them) and He healed them. When most of the people were against the tax collectors and rich people who took advantage on the poor, He spent time with these people and showed them how wrong they were, taught them His ways of treating other human beings. The Scribes, Pharisees and other religious zealots despised Jesus for spending time and identifying Himself with these people.

Jesus was human and sensing the antagonistic spirit against Him daily, it is recorded in the Gospels that Jesus withdrew Himself from the masses of people and He went to the top of the mountains, hills valleys and the Garden Gethsemane and He prayed many days and nights. He wanted to spend time with His Father God, here is where He found sustenance and strength daily to live and do what He came to do. Jesus was also lonely and, in His loneliness, keeping company with His Father and having fellowship with His Father God, was His only source of strength and Help.

Jesus experienced loneliness more than anyone else, before His Crucifixion He took the eleven Apostles to go and pray with Him in the Garden of Gethsemane. Judas's betrayal of Jesus, the echo of the footsteps of Roman soldiers rumbling and vibrating nearby, then sensing the agony of the Cross. Jesus obviously being human felt the pangs of pains of being crucified. The only source of strength He could obtain was from His Father, God, was to pray. His disciples whom He carried to pray with Him fell asleep in His greatest hour of need, (just like today, it's a miracle if you can find anyone to pray with you in your hour of need) when the Roman soldiers arrested Jesus not one the disciples could be found for a while.

Talk about loneliness! This was loneliness to the core. But God and only God was His source of strength. This is the reason He prayed like He did in the Garden of Gethsemane. This is where He whopped the antagonism of the religious zealots of that day, the agonizing prayer He prayed in the Garden of Gethsemane his sweat were as drops of blood which came from his body. But the prayer He prayed at that moment strengthened Him for entire ordeal of trial, whipping, carrying the Cross and being crucified.

BEFORE AND AFTER PRAYER, MAINTAIN A PURE HEART A RIGHT SPIRIT TOWARDS GOD AND TO OTHERS,

lonely people can develop a filthy heart, dirty minds and wild imaginations. Generally speaking, this in itself is self destructive. God cannot help anyone with impure hearts and spirits. Help is what is needed especially in loneliness, but no one not even God can help when an individual's mind, heart and spirit is corroded with all type of impurities. If God is going to help in particular lonely people, people with all types of problems. It is important to maintain a pure heart and right spirit always. This is why the Psalmist and King David of the Bible, prayed this prayer *in Psalm 51: 4, create within me a right spirit and a pure heart Oh God.* God can only answer prayer and help an individual when they maintain a pure heart and a right spirit.

MAINTAIN A SPIRIT OF THANKFULLNESS AND PRAISE TOWARDS GOD,

a thankful person is a happy person. Worship and praise to God is of utmost importance. People who are thankful have a tendency to be content. Thankfulness ushers an individual into worship and praise towards God. Worship and praise is not just being in a church to sing, shout and hear the choir sing, and the rendering of special music, this is commendable and should be encouraged. But thankfulness, praise and worship is something that a person can do all by themselves, and this can be done from the moment a person wakes up in the morning, through out the day and before going to bed at night. How can this be done? By an individual opening their mouth and saying God I thank you, I praise you I worship you and this can be done constantly when by yourself, this will make a difference in your life.

Worship and praise towards God is power, power to overcome every problem, situations and circumstances. Thankfulness, worship and praise go together all of these three is an offering in a way that is acceptable unto God which produces a better spirit within an individual. Worship is also bringing an offering to God.

BEFORE, DURING AND AFTER PRAYER, MAINTAIN AN UNWEAVERING FAITH IN GOD AND A SPIRIT OF EXPENTANCY,

there was a time in America that some people would look as Christians as some kind religious freaks, fanatics and fanatizas. But within the past years people who does not have any idea of Christianity, they are beginning to notice with an uncomfortable feeling deep down inside of them, their home, surroundings, town, city, State they live. and the entire world does not feel like it use to feel. Some of them touted, laughed and even had the attitude towards Christians, well! Why the Bible? Why all the talk about God, going to Church, the praying and other activities within Christian Circles.

Exclaimed! A certain individual I am puzzled and troubled by the signs, sights, catastrophes, hate with the intention to kill and destroy, wars, famine, earthquakes, dissident's movements, the ungodly lifestyle and much more. This same individual spoke these words which caught my attention "*I have nothing to hang on to*" then I spoke right back with God's love within my being and said these words "*with all that is going on at this present time I have something some one and some thijng to hang on too, FAITH IN GOD*". Millions of people at this present time are mesmerized and troubled by what is happening at this present time, which is producing a troubled and a lonely feeling inside of them. Faith in God combined with prayer and expecting your prayers to be answered gives a feeling of self confidence and safety.

How to pray, desire to pray, taking time to pray, finding a place to pray, reading the Bible, spending time with God, telling Him about your problems, needs, situations, God wants us to come to Him, and in God alone through Jesus Christ and the power of the Holy Spirit you will find help. Even lonely people, God is you're only comfort and hope. Some of the most inspiring words in the Bible are these:

God is our refuge and strength a very present time trouble

Therefore, we will not fear

Even though the earth be removed

And though the mountains be carried into the midst of the sea

Though the waters roar and be troubled

Though the mountains shake with its swelling

There is a river whose streams shall make glad the city of God

The Holy Place of the Tabernacle of the Most High

God is in the midst of her she shall not be moved

God shall her just at the break of down

The Nations raged the kingdom were moved

He uttered His Voice the earth melted

The Lord of host is with us, the God of Jacob is our refuge

Come behold the works of the Lord

Who hath made desolations in the earth?

He makes wars to cease to the end of the earth

He breaks the bow and cuts the spear in two

He burns the chariots with fire

Be still and know I am God

I will be exalted among the Nations

I will be exalted in the Earth,

Psalm 46

God in Jesus Name Bless the Reader of This Book

Whatever problems they are going through

Especially those who are suffering from loneliness

Help and Minister to them through the power of the Holy Spirit

In Jesus Name: Amen.

THE END

www.ingramcontent.com/pod-product-compliance
Lightning Source LLC
Chambersburg PA
CBHW060532130626
46553CB00002B/717